TOM BROWN'S
SYNDICALISM

Tom Brown
Tom Brown's Syndicalism

0 948984 16 3
JULY 1990

Phoenix Press
PO Box 824
London
N1 9DL

Cover by Kathleen Blakistone
Typeset by San Fairy Ann
Printed in Great Britain by BPCC Wheatons Ltd, Exeter

Contents

ABOUT TOM BROWN

Tom Brown, whose writings did much to revive interest in Syndicalism and Workers' Control, was that rare phenomenon in the British libertarian movement, a theoretician whose ideas had been tested and developed by his own experience in the hard school of working-class struggle.

An able and persuasive public speaker, whether at Speakers' Corner in Hyde Park, at indoor meetings, or in the more intimate role of lecturer, he had the happy knack of relating what he said to the everyday experience of his audience. The same quality illuminated his writings, which mirrored the life and times of this lifelong revolutionary and loyal comrade.

Born and bred within sight and sound of the Tyneside shipyards, Tom served his engineering apprenticeship there and was quickly drawn into militant industrial activity. Much of his working life was spent as an active shop steward and factory floor activist.

Like many others he was fired with enthusiasm by the Russian Revolution, was an early member of the Communist Party and, for a time, became its industrial organiser for the North East. But the double dealing of the CP and the growing repression in Bolshevik Russia quickly brought disillusion and he left the party, though never his natural role as a shop floor militant.

Moving south during the Depression, he worked in the motor industry of the West Midlands and, probably around this time, was attracted by Anarchist and Syndicalist ideas. In the mid-thirties he and his wife, Lily, found their way further south to London with their daughters, Ruth and Grace.

The Spanish Revolution of 1936, with its takeover of industry and agriculture by the Syndicalist unions of the CNT in anti-fascist territory, especially Catalonia, reinforced and developed Tom's own ideas and he became a member of the grouping around the paper, 'Spain and the World', which was dedicated to supporting the Spanish workers . He spoke at meetings supporting their struggle, several times sharing the platform with Emma Goldman. His Syndicalist writings appeared for the first time in 'Revolt', which followed 'Spain and the World' after Franco's fascist victory in 1939.

During the war, as a member of the Anarchist Federation of Britain (AFB), he wrote regularly for 'War Commentary for Anarchism' and produced his first two pamphlets, 'Trade Unionism or Syndicalism' and 'The British General Strike', both of which had wide sales. He remained a member of the editorial board until near the end of the war, when the AFB, of which he stayed an active member, parted company with Freedom Press in unhappy circumstances, but on points of principle.

With others, he helped launch 'Direct Action' in 1945, as the AFB's new voice and continued his close association with it for well over 20 years. Saddened by the failure of an attempt to form an International of Anarchist Federations in the late 1940s, he later supported the AFB's decision to change its name to Syndicalist Workers' Federation (SWF) and affiliate to the International Working Men's Association, of which the CNT was the strongest member, although then underground in Spain. The SWF maintained friendly contacts with the IWW in the States and Tom visited them when he and Lily crossed the Atlantic to see their daughters, who had both married GIs in London and later emigrated. He also went to see the veteran Anarcho-Syndicalist, Rudolf Rocker, in a libertarian colony near New York. Tom and Lily returned to London after a year and he resumed his SWF activity. He and Lily, who was then in poor health, returned to Tyneside in the late 1960s and his continued activity there included several lively contributions, on libertarian subjects, on local radio.

Tom Brown's activity and writings influenced and inspired many people. A latter-day Tom Mann, he sowed the seeds of a rebirth for Syndicalism in this country.

Trade Unionism Or Syndicalism?

War increases the necessity of working-class organisation, for with the rapid rise in the cost of living and the power of the government real wages fall and working conditions worsen. This is the time chosen by the trade union bureaucrats to make a Judas bargain with the employer. A truce to the struggle for wages and the sacrifice of every trade union gain of the last 80 years. The trade union leaders are seeking to make the unions a sort of British Nazi Labour Front, but they have nothing to learn from Herr Ley.

We cannot explain the decline of militant unionism simply by attacking the leaders. There have been many successful attacks on Right-wing leaders and their replacement by Lefts and Communists. Shortly afterwards the Lefts and Communists have been bitterly attacked by their previous supporters for being even more reactionary than their predecessors. We must examine the ideas and structure of trade unionism; the leadership is but the natural fruit of the movement -' men do not gather figs of thorns or grapes of thistles.'

Syndicalism alone gives a constructive criticism of trade unionism.

Craft or Industrial Unionism?

Most of the early unions of the British workers were trade or craft unions; that is, they organised men according to the tools they used. If a man used certain woodworking tools, he joined a carpenter's union, slightly different tools would put him into another organisation. The unhappy result is that men in one factory, under one roof, and working together to produce one commodity, find themselves 'organised' in a score of unions, because they use different tools (the engineering industry alone has over 50 unions). Constant quarrels over poaching of members and demarcation arise. Even inter-union strikes have taken place. This method of organisation may have been justified in the Middle Ages, when a craftsman often produced a whole commodity by his own tools and labour, but it is obviously outdated in the 20th century, when dozens of trades, each subdivided and assisted or guided by technicians, clerks, storemen, and others combine in the production of even the simplest commodities.

Equally unfortunate are the younger unions - the general workers, such as the Transport and General Workers' Union. These unions seek to organise everyone without regard to any sort of working or other relationship. All go into a higgledy-piggledy mass, so that a metal worker on the same job as a member of the Amalgamated Engineering Union, will find himself in the same union as tram conductors and farm workers; or a docker will be in the Municipal Workers' Union.

Syndicalism declares for *industrial,* not craft unionism. All workers in one factory, all producing the same commodity, should be in one union; all crafts, the unskilled and the semi-skilled, the clerks, the technicians, the women, and the youth. While the trade unions cry' 100 per cent trades unionism ' the craft unions exclude from membership 50 per cent of the population - the womenfolk - and divide the 'organised' workers among a thousand unions while about twenty-five unions would be sufficient. ONE INDUSTRY ONE UNION.

Doss House Organising

Syndicalism organises the union branch at the place of employment. Most unions (the miners are an exception) form their branches near their members' homes. If a man works in Poplar and sleeps in Willesden, he joins a Willesden branch of his union. The unions are organised like doss-houses - they ask not where you work, but where you sleep. Now the worker's problems arise at his place of employment; there he can discuss with his mates the questions of factory safety or sanitation, piece-work scales, wages, or the tyranny of some petty overseer. But in his trade union branch he may not meet any work-mate. In the engineering union he may meet fellow members working in varied industries, chemical, power, ship-building, or transport; in many other unions it is even more varied. To sustain the greatest interest and militancy take the union branch to the job.

Coffin Clubs

The failure of the trade unions as fighting organisations is partly due to their friendly society character. They pay out sick, superannuation, unemployment, and death benefits, tasks now undertaken by the State. They have become not militant working class bodies, but coffin clubs. In the craft unions most of the contributions (often 2 shillings a week) and most of the energy of the organisation go to this end. Now the paying of friendly society benefits entails the accumulation of large funds. The existence of such funds means Investment - Capital. Investment in property, investment in capitalist enterprises which exploit their workers for

8

profits, investment in WAR LOAN. These funds give the unions an interest in the welfare of capitalism which paralyses their activities as fighting bodies. The officials and the more timid members who hope to draw benefits fear a strike which might imperil the funds. Cut out the coffin club and a union can be run on a membership contribution of threepence or fourpence a week. It may be said that high contributions mean big strike funds and are a financial guarantee of militant action; but only a small proportion of the funds are paid out in strike benefit. In any case most strikes in the last thirteen years have been (and all strikes are now) unofficial and no money is paid out of union funds. But the absence of a war chest does not necessarily mean no strike. Some of the most bitter and desperate strikes have been fought on empty cash boxes. At the end of April 1926 most of the miners' unions entered the strike with about one week's strike pay in hand; yet they continued the fight for over nine months. Let us never forget that the comparatively wealthy unions of Germany succumbed to Fascism without a struggle, while the poor unions of Spain for nearly three years fought the whole world of capitalism. The possession of property does not make one a fighter, but often brings the fear of losing that property. A human failing Hitler has thoroughly exploited.

Climbing the Social Ladder

One reason for the existence of the 'Labour Leader' type is the high rate of salaries paid by the workers to their leaders; salaries supplemented by taking on extra jobs, speaking or writing for the capitalist press. Their income puts them in another class. They eat different food, live in better houses, attend Ascot and Royal Garden parties, their wives are introduced to titled women, and generally they live in a new world. Any sympathy they had for the workers dies. Their hopes are not for an equalitarian society, but for higher salaries. Listen to a frank member of the species: in the Daily Express of June 6th, 1939, Mr. W. J. Brown, General Secretary of the Civil Service Clerical Association, writes: ' Among the relatively underpaid classes in Britain are the Trade Union leaders. I earn £1,000 a year. Sir Walter Citrine, the secretary of the Trades Union Congress, also gets £1,000 a year. Mr. Ernest Bevin gets £1,250 a year. Mr. Marchbank of the National Union of Railwaymen gets £1,000 a year.' Just to show us what he is aiming at he quotes the salaries attached to a few 'comparative' jobs. Green of the American Federation of Labour and his rival Lewis of the Congress of Industrial Organizations get about £5,000 a year each. Next the Civil Service bureaucrats: £3,500 for Sir

9

Warren Fisher, but for Sir Horace Wilson (the Government Labour advisor)' a beggarly £3,000 a year.' On to the company directors: Lord Stamp, £20,000; Lord Ashfield (London Passenger Transport Board), £12,500; and Lord Cowan of Imperial Chemicals is reputed to get some £70,000 a year. Says W. J. Brown' Is there any hope that the anomalies will be ironed out? Very little. Trade Union memberships behave sometimes as if they had no hearts.'

Organisers and secretaries should be paid the district rate of wages of their members, and there should be only the minimum of paid organisers. After all in the trade unions some of the most necessary work is done without pay by shop-stewards and others on the job. Organising, recruiting and struggling for better conditions. If those who envy Lord Ashfield leave us we have lost nothing, we still have the stalwarts who believe.

Trade Unions and the State

A truly working class organisation can never collaborate with the State as do the trade unions. When the unions were first formed the State persecuted them, now it has won them over and incorporated them in the machinery of the State. Trade unions administer State health insurance and their representatives sit on Government committees from Labour Exchange committees which chop unemployment benefit to Royal Commissions for suppressing colonial workers. The trade union bosses even appear on the Honours List. The Versaille Treaty, which made the present war inevitable, bears the signature of a Labour representative, G. N. Barnes of the Amalgamated Engineering Union. Even the conscientious objector finds himself confronted by a tribunal with a trade union representative. How ironical a jest that a labour leader should be an arbiter of conscience!

But the State is nothing but the executive committee of the ruling class and no one can serve the workers and serve the employers. Now we see a trade union leader, Ernest Bevin, as Minister of Labour introducing industrial conscription. Workers are forbidden to leave their jobs for new employment but may be forcibly transferred to other localities at the whim of the employers or Mr. Bevin's department. Sometimes workers are allowed to leave only to find themselves unable to gain Mr. Bevin's permission to work and after a few weeks impoverishment, just to teach them that escape is impossible, they are forced back to their old work. Yet still fatheads are found who murmur: 'It's just as well to have a few of your own men in the Government.'

Syndicalism has no friends in the Government.

10

Every advance by trade unionists, or even by unorganised workers has been gained by a strike or the threat of a strike; that is, by the willingness to withdraw one's labour power. Even an individual threat to quit the job is an application of the strike weapon. Trade unions owe their birth and growth to the strike. Now they have abandoned it for parliamentary activity and class collaboration their spirit has perished though their form may linger on.

It is often said that Parliament and the Government have given higher wages or a shorter working day to the workers. This is only apparent. In 1919 the miners of Britain demanded higher wages and a national six hour day, demands they could have enforced, for British coal was in great demand, even at £6 a ton. The coal owners could not afford a stoppage. The miners were quieted by a Royal Commission and an Act of Parliament, which gave them a wages advance and a seven hour day, less than they might have enforced. (The miners of the North of England already worked less than the seven hour day.) But in 1921, when economic conditions were unfavourable and the miners' organisation weakened, the wage advances were lost. In 1926, after the miners had been defeated on the economic field, Parliament scrapped the seven hour day for an eight hour day.

Trade Boards usually 'fix' wages at or below the market rate of labour. If the market falls, then the Trade Board rate is quite often dodged by workers, driven to accept a job below rates, and by employers, who 'forget' to pay the proper rate of wages, and who only remember if an inspector calls, succumbing to amnesia a few weeks later. This is particularly true of the cheap clothing trade. An overstocked labour market and a weak economic organisation of the workers always mean lower wages.

The Lightning Strike

However, the Syndicalist defence of the strike weapon does not mean approval of the trade union method of striking, which usually fails. Syndicalism uses many variations of the strike, but it is possible here only to mention a few. Perhaps the commonest Syndicalist weapon is the 'lightning strike.' Before a trade union strikes long negotiations take place, six months notice is given, and the strike is postponed a few months. Then when, and only when, the employer and the government have prepared huge reserves of commodities or transport, and have organised police and blacklegs, the strike takes place. Agreements are made in such a way as to ensure this by long period notices and district agreements. (The miners' district agreements have always been made to ensure a striking district

11

being defeated by all the other districts.) Of course, the labour leaders regard all such agreements as sacred, but if the workers are to win their blows must be sudden and in the unexpected place. Speed and surprise are essential to victory.

Almost equally important is the 'guerrilla strike,' to wage a struggle in any section of an industry, in any locality or even in a single factory, wherever conditions may be temporarily favourable, but the highly centralised trade union movement cannot do this. Some industries, particularly engineering, vary in prosperity - aircraft may be booming, locomotive building declining - yet wage rates are determined by the condition of railway engineering. The lowest wage becomes the highest.

If the workers in a prosperous branch of industry see a chance to strike successfully, they must seek permission of the leaders at the national centre of the union. Of course, the leaders are not in sympathy, permission is refused, and the opportunity is lost.

The Syndicalist method is not organisation from the top down but from the bottom upward. Each branch is allowed local autonomy but all branches are federated into districts, all districts into a national federation of labour. This is federalism, the opposite of bureaucratic centralism.

Federalism also makes possible the sympathetic strike. Under centralism one union blacklegs another. When the iron moulders went on strike, trade union machinists and fitters continued work, helping to break the strike. When the London busmen struck in 1937, the petrol 'busmen and trolleybus drivers, *members of the same union* broke the strike.

Syndicalism federates the workers into one force, where each unit is ready to support the other. The preamble of the Industrial Workers of the World well said: An injury to one is the concern of all.

The Boycott

The boycott has been little used by unions, apart from the Syndicalist unions of Spain and Scandinavia. Here is a mighty weapon, but one that does not cause the loss of wages of the common strike. It is of course best applied to those trades relying on the workers' purchasing power. To support the claims of the employees the workers are organised to withdraw patronage of certain chain stores, cinemas, cafes, or branded goods. The term 'boycott' has lost much of its terror since the days when it was used by the Irish Land League. The League was the poor peasants' defence against the landlord. When a landlord evicted a tenant farmer the League applied its boycott against the new tenant and the landlord. Domestic servants left their houses, the labourers their fields and cattle, the grocer, the butcher, and even the doctor refused to serve them. The

12

boycott was the most effective weapon ever used by the Irish peasantry. But the method can (in our complex economic society) even more effectively be used by the organised industrial workers.

'Work to Rule'

Many ingenious strike tactics have been invented by the French Syndicalists. Of these the' work to rule' of the railwaymen (on a few occasions copied by the English railwaymen) is the best known. Thousands of laws and rules for running the railways are made by the directors and government. Of course most of them are unused and even unknown, their place being taken by common sense and daily experience of the job. When the French railwaymen were forbidden to strike their Anarchist fellow-workers were delighted to point out to them the absurdity of the law, so the Anarcho-syndicalists decided carefully to fulfil the law. The railway laws were carried out just as the government said they ought to be. One French law demands the driver to make sure of the safety of the train before crossing a bridge. So express engine drivers stopped their trains at every bridge to consult the guard. The expresses were late. A favourite rule of militant railwaymen was that which said that tickets must be examined on both sides. The rule says nothing of city rush hours. The results of working to rule were to tie up the railways, make the law look an ass, and win the railwaymen's cause.

A somewhat similar Syndicalist tactic used on the continent was the 'good work strike.' Workers building cheap working class houses would put their very best workmanship into the shoddy materials. Doors hung straight, windows opened, roofs were waterproof, and walls were perpendicular.

The most amusing case of this form of strike action is surely that of the accusation against the I. W. W. section operating in a salmon-canning plant. It was said that they stuck cheap labels on the most expensive cuts of salmon. From the poor districts of the world came new orders for salmon and from the better-off bitter rebukes.

The Social Strike

All Anarcho-Syndicalist strikes are not intended to protect some section of workers or raise wages by a few shillings. Some are intended to rally all the workers in defence of their class interests, and some transcend even class interests and defend humanity. The *social strike* has been used

13

against war, as in the Catalonian workers' general strike against the Moroccan war in July, 1909, and in the German armament workers' congress in Erfurt which decided to make no more war weapons to destroy men, but to compel their employers to convert their factories to produce useful commodities. The resolution of the German workers was maintained for two years until broken by the orthodox trade unions. The Anarcho-Syndicalist workers of Sommerda held out until their jobs were taken by members of the trade unions. Had the trade unions of the world supported and copied this brave action, Hitler and the Second World War would not have been.

Another good example of the social strike comes from Spain. Some years ago the Spanish government wished to build a womens' prison in Barcelona. The building workers of Catalonia refused to build it. In vain the governments sought workers from other parts of Spain, the prison site remained untouched until foreign labour was imported.

'Stay-In Strikes'

All these ways of striking are but skirmishes before the real battle; training for the most powerful of Syndicalist weapons - the stay-in strike. The workers, instead of leaving the factories or other plant in their employers' hands to be used for blacklegging, stay in the plant and lock-out the employers. The plan is blackleg-proof and protects the strikers. To baton them the employers must first smash their own property.

A few examples will show the efficacy of this weapon. In the U. S. A. the automobile workers had suffered many defeats until in 1937 they staged a 'stay-in strike' and victory was theirs.

In 1936 the French workers found their wages falling. The factory workers seized the factories and were quickly followed by millions of others, even the sales girls of the fashionable shops. By their action they won wage increases, holidays with pay, the forty hour week, and many other gains. Unfortunately, shortly afterwards the workers helped into power a 'Popular Front' of Liberals, Socialist Party and Communists. Almost immediately the Popular Front Government began to filch the gains of May, 1936, to introduce industrial conscription and prepare the path of French Fascism.

In Italy in 1920 the metalworkers were to be locked-out for refusing a reduction in wages. Instead they locked-out the employers. The strike was everywhere successful. Supported by the railwaymen, the bakers and other workers, the engineers lacked nothing. Unfortunately, the workers handed back the factories in return for increased wages.

Since then lies have been invented to create a picture of disorder.

Listen, however, to a celebrated journalist, George Seldes in *Sawdust Cae-sar*...'.Not a safe was cracked. Not a skull....Commotion everywhere except in Italy. It is true that day by day more and more factories were being occupied by the workers. Soon 500,000 'strikers' were at work building automobiles, steamships, forging tools, manufacturing a thousand useful things, but there was not a shop or factory owner there to boss them or to dictate letters in the vacant offices. Peace reigned.'

'There is not a socialist in the world today who can indicate with any degree of clearness how we can bring about the co-operative commonwealth except along the lines suggested by industrial organisation of the workers.

Political institutions are not adapted to the administration of industry. Only industrial organisations are adapted to the administration of a co-operative commonwealth that we are working for. Only the industrial form of organisation offers us even a theoretical constructive socialist programme. There is no constructive socialism except on the industrial field.' (James Connolly quoting from *The Wage Slave*.)

The greatest weakness of the trade union is its lack of an ultimate aim, a supreme reason for existence. At its best it struggles for a higher wage or a shorter working day. (At its worst it gives up that struggle.) But a struggling man usually has some aim. He intends to end his struggle victoriously by finally overcoming his enemy, not to keep the action going for ever and ever. So the ultimate aim of Syndicalism is not a wage increase, but the abolition of the wage system. Every action by the Syndicalist workers is a means to that end. Every strike is a training period, a skirmish before the social general strike. (Of course, some trade unions have a vague paragraph about socialism in the preambles of their rule books, but it does not affect their conduct, which cannot be other than conservative.)

So the aim of the revolutionary Syndicalists in the stay-in strikes in France, Italy and elsewhere has always been to persuade the workers to keep on holding the factories and other plants, never to return them for promises.

The spontaneity of the movement can ensure its success. Railmen run trucks to the factory sidings. Bakers bake the strikers' bread. Telephonists transmit their messages. All syndicates are linked in mutual support.

15

The Fascist Danger

The timid say: 'If the workers control industry the employing-class will hire bands of Fascists to shoot the workers and regain the factories. Better to trust the ballot box.' How is it the ruling class has the power to bribe? They obtain their wealth from industry, and if they no longer control industry their source of profit dries, their accumulated paper money is worthless and their bank balances are unrealised. Their control of the press and other technical means of propaganda lost, they can no longer manufacture 'public opinion'.

'The Fascists will shoot and bayonet the workers,' but who makes the rifles, bullets and bayonets - who handles them first?

Surely, the workers. Who must transport the Fascists and their supplies? Who feed them, supply their water, gas, power, every need of life? Always, the workers. In this modern, complicated society no power can exist without the co-operation of the workers. The power is in their hands.

It is often said that the Italian workers were turned out of the factories in the 1920 strike by the Italian Fascists. This is pure invention. During that strike the Fascists, the police and the authorities were helpless. The workers voluntarily vacated the factories in return for temporary gains. Mussolini, to win popularity, applauded their action. The Fascist seizure of power did not take place until 1922.

It is impossible to close this chapter without asking the Social-Democrats: if the workers are defenceless when they control factories, railways, ships, power stations and all the life-blood of society, how can they conquer when their only weapon is a slip of ballot-paper marked with a politician's name?

The Framework of a New Society

Workers' control of industry by the Syndicalist method would be exercised industry by industry. Thus the engineering industry would be run by engineers, technicians, mechanics, machinists and all others; the building trade by builders, the printing trade by printers and so on. Each factory, mill, mine or job would have its regular assembly of workers and its department and factory committees elected by the workers in that plant. All factories in one industry would be federated into a district industrial federation with a district council, such as the Midland Engineers' Federation, or the Yorkshire Textile Federation.

All districts of each industry would be federated into a national

16

federation until there were organisations of all the twenty-five or so industries. Delegates of the national industrial federations would form a National Council of Labour co-ordinating the whole economy of the country.

While all industry would be linked, each plant would have autonomy over its particular affairs, the general business of the industry being dealt with by the district or national committees. Control would be exercised from the bottom up. To prevent the divorce of committee-men from the masses it would be necessary to change the committee personnel at fairly frequent intervals. None would be the worse for a refresher course at the bench or machine. Also, the members of committees would be delegates, not representatives, as are Members of Parliament. They would be expected to interpret the views of their fellows, rather than expound their own pet fancies. Of course, they would be subject to recall. Those who elect should be able to cancel their choice. It is a right every employer claims.

Workers' Control versus State Control

It is often asked: 'but if you have an economic control instead of a political, who will run the hospitals?' Who but the health workers, doctors, nurses and others are capable of running them? The politicians and lawyers? In the same way the schools would be managed by the teachers, who have studied education, not by successful grocers, publicans and estate agents. The state performs no useful function that could not be carried out by the Syndicates.

Syndicalism has nothing in common with Nationalisation - that is State Capitalism. Under capitalism the workers do not own or control the means of production, so they are forced to work for wages. Under state capitalism or nationalisation they do not control but work for wages and are exploited for profit. How does the Post Office obtain its huge profits but from the exploitation of its employees, in many cases very poorly paid?

Nationalisation brings no new liberty to the worker; instead he finds his life controlled by the bureaucracy. He cannot leave one employer to seek a higher bidder for his labour power. There is only one employer, the merciless state. There is no effective protest against the muddle, inefficiency or cruelty of a state bureaucracy. Every official denies his responsibility: it is some other official. The protestor is handed from one official to another and back again until he drops from sheer exhaustion.

Parliament and Government are unsuited to the running of industry. A member of Parliament claims to represent all his constituents, who may be builders, weavers, engineers, miners or 'bus drivers, all of whom have

17

different work problems. He just cannot do it. An engineer should be delegate of the engineers, a textile worker of the weavers. The managing of industry is a technical job, requiring special knowledge, but no provision for each industry is made in Parliament. It is possible, by a freak of chance, for Parliament to be composed entirely of retired generals or lawyers. The State was born to make and enforce laws protecting private property. Socialism is not a political system but an economic method and an economic system requires economic organisation.

A Lesson from Spain

Once it was possible for the dyspeptic cynic to say: 'All that is a beautiful dream but it isn't possible.' We have now the example of the Spanish workers' collectivisation during the civil war of 1936-39. It proved the possibility and the regenerative powers of workers' control of industry.

Upon the outbreak of the civil war many of the industries and most of the land were taken by the syndicates of workers and peasants and run with the greatest success. In Catalonia the railways were administered by joint committees of the Anarcho-syndicalist C. N. T. and the socialist trade union U. G. T. while in Barcelona the 'buses, trams and underground were taken over by the C. N. T. In Barcelona control was also exercised by Syndicates of Health, Water, Gas, Amusements and many others. In other parts of Spain outstanding examples of socialisation were the textile industry of Alcoy, and the woodworking industry in Cuenca and other towns.

The most outstanding successes were in agriculture, where the big estates were taken by the landless peasants, and where most of the small peasants formed voluntary collectives. This resulted not only in betterment of the landworkers' economic position, but also in greater agricultural efficiency. Better seed and stock were selected, more machinery, such as tractors, were used, and general production increased. Schools were formed (each of the 500 collectives had its own school) and homes for the aged were founded. Doctors were sent to every village and clinics were organised by the Health Workers' Syndicate. Mutual aid took the place of 'charity' and beggary.

The Revolution of Construction

The opponents of Anarchism often tell us we cannot have Anarchism overnight. We know that well. Everything must be built up, but the time

18

to start building is now. As previous societies decayed there developed within them the embryo of new forms of societies, so within capitalism we build the framework of socialism: the Syndicates.

From every struggle and from our daily work we must learn how to run industries and services. We must develop the class-consciousness, the knowledge and self-confidence of the workers, until the embryonic society bursts the shell of capitalism. As the I. W. W. preamble put it: 'By organising industrially we are forming the new society within the shell of the old.'

Capitalism threatens to destroy society with itself, and the only force that can save humanity is the revolutionary workers. The Anarchists call the workers to the Syndicalist revolution: *Revolution of Construction.*

The British General Strike 1926

Storm Clouds

In the spring of 1925 storm clouds gathered over the British coalfields. The coming struggle was the chief conversational topic in the grim mining villages. Germany was re-entering the international trade war as a competitor of Britain. The German miners' wages had been slashed, the industry rationalised by the aid of Anglo-American capital investment, German currency stabilised by the Dawes plan. Already faced by this keen competitor, the British coal export trade was embarrassed by the Governments's return to the Gold Standard.

It was soon obvious that the mine owners would meet the new international situation by cutting wages and on June 30, 1925, they served notice to terminate the national agreement, proposing ending the minimum wage, heavy wage cuts and district, instead of national agreements. The Miners' Federation of Great Britain replied by putting their case before the Trades Union Congress General Council at a joint meeting on July 10. The General Council pledged the trade unions to full support of the miners and, setting up a Special Committee, met the executives of all the railway and transport unions, who agreed upon an embargo on moving coal. The unions quickly acted by issuing 'Official Instructions to all Railway and Transport Workers:'

"Wagons containing coal must not be attached to any train after midnight on Friday, July 31, and after this time wagons of coal must not be supplied to any industrial or commercial concerns. . . .(Coal exports): All tippers and trimmers will cease work at the end of the second shift on July 31. (Coal Imports): On no account may import coal be handled from July 31. . . .All men engaged in delivering coal to commercial and industrial concerns will cease Friday night, July 31.'

A specially summoned conference of trade union executive committees gave unanimous support to the instructions.

Unprepared for such resistance, the Cabinet, which had fiercely backed the coal-owners, hastily met and the Prime Minister (Baldwin) summoned the leaders of miners and owners to Downing Street. On the morning of Friday, July 31, the government announced the granting of a subsidy to the coal industry amounting to £25,000,000 and extending over nine months. The wage cuts and other demands of the owners were postponed until April, 1926. July 31, 1925 became known as 'Red Friday.'

It was obvious to all that the nine months' grace was

20

merely a time of preparation for the ruling class and this thought was expressed in the report of the Special Committee of the T. U. C. It felt that its task had not been completed, and with the consent of the General Council proposed to remain in being, and to apply itself to the task of devising ways and means of consolidating the resistance of the trade union movement should the attack be renewed.

Alas! Little, if any, preparation for the inevitable struggle was made by the T. U. C. or the affiliated unions. Not so the Government. Speaking of Red Friday, Winston Churchill, then Chancellor of the Exchequer, said: 'We therefore decided to postpone the crisis in the hope of averting it, or if not of averting it, of coping effectually with it when the time comes.'

A strike-breaking organisation known as O. M. S. (Organisation for the Maintenance of Supplies) was created. Blacklegs were trained to drive locomotives in the private railways of large factories at week-ends and potential scabs instructed in the operation of telephones and telegraphy. The country was placed on a war footing by dividing it into ten areas, each under a Civil Commissioner, and a civil service organisation was set up in each of these areas. Great numbers of special constables were enrolled and mobile squads of police organised. Every possible preparation was made and the Commissioners and their officers stood ready for the signal.

In the meantime a Royal Commission on the Coal Industry, presided over by Sir Herbert Samuel, presented its report. The report was vague and woolly on the subject of re-organisation of the industry, but very definite in demanding wage reductions and the lengthening of the working day.

On the First of May

As the renewal of the battle became more certain, the miners rallied around the slogan 'Not a penny off the pay, not a minute on the day, no district agreements,' and behind the leadership of the indefatigible A. J. Cook attempted to arouse the Labour Movement.

In April the coalowners announced that unless the miners accepted the employers' demands a lock-out would take place on May 1. On April 20, King George V proclaimed a 'State of Emergency' and the Special Constabulary were mobilised. Hyde Park became a military camp, troops in full war kit paraded the streets and tanks and armoured cars rumbled into Newcastle, Liverpool, Birmingham and all the industrial cities. Warships were sent up the Thames, the Tyne, the Humber and the Clyde.

The executives of the trade unions were called to a conference of the T. U. C. on April 29. The conference continued to sit during the following day (Friday) while the T. U. C. leaders trotted to and fro between the conference hall and Downing Street, begging Baldwin to find a way out. Said J. H. Thomas: 'I suppose my usual critics will say that Thomas was almost grovelling, and it is true. . . .I never begged and pleaded like I begged and pleaded all today.'

Saturday, May 1, 1926 - May Day - one million miners were locked out. The T. U. C. conference assembled at forenoon in the Memorial Hall, Farringdon Street, and received the General Strike Memorandum of the General Council. A tense pause and the roll call began, union by union. For once in a score of years a trade union conference expressed the mood of the workers. For the General Strike - 3,653,527; against - 49,911; unable to reply in time - 318,000. The executive rose and sang the 'Red Flag 'and left the gloomy old hall for the sunshine of the streets, to mingle with the greatest May Day demonstration London had ever seen. Strange though it seems, the T. U. C. leaders immediately resumed their begging perambulations to Downing Street. While still trying to avert the strike, they were suddenly horrified to learn the fight had already started. Late on Sunday night, May 2, the leaders of the Miners' Federation and the T. U. C. were meeting the full Cabinet at Downing Street when the news of the first skirmish reached them. The *Daily Mail* was about to appear with a particularly vicious anti-strike article. The type had already been set and moulded, the machines set up and the proof copies run off. When the machinists read the bitter words of editorial hatred of the workers, the machines stopped, the Natsopa chapel met and quickly decided to tell the management to delete the leader if they wanted their paper. All other departments met and decided to back the machine room. Monday, May 3 and no *Daily Mail* appeared.

When Baldwin heard the news he jumped up from the table and ended the negotiations. The T. U. C. leaders still grovelled to avoid the fight. Said one of the most prominent grovellers:

'With other union leaders, I sought an interview with the Prime Minister and his colleagues in a last-minute attempt to show that the compositors' strike was isolated and unofficial, without our approval, and to plead, almost on our knees, for a less cruel arbitration than he was forcing upon us - an open fight between the workers and the Cabinet. But the Cabinet had left Number 10, and the place was deserted save by a single sleepy attendant.' (*Memoirs:* J. R. Clynes.)

Think of it - a general repudiating his soldiers on the eve of battle and condemning them for being ready to fight!

In the House of Commons the grovelling went on, but the Government knew the cowardice of the labour leaders and refused to allow them

22

a way out. Baldwin knew the T. U. C. and Labour Party leaders hated and feared the General Strike.

'He (Baldwin) turned on us and quoted an article written some time before by Ramsay MacDonald in *The New Leader*: 'All my life I have been opposed to the sympathetic strike. It has no practical value; it has one certain result - a blinding reaction. Liberty is far more easily destroyed by those who abuse it than by those who oppose it.'

'I agree with every word of that,' commented Baldwin to the hushed and crowded House.' (*Memoirs*, J. R. Clynes)

So Baldwin led the employers to battle with an I. L. P. text inscribed on their banners. Midnight, Monday, May 3, 1926, the General Strike was on.

Lions Led By Rats

Britain awoke on the morning of Tuesday, May 4, to find the General Strike in being. The railways were still and silent, buses and trams had disappeared, no newspaper was on sale. Unfortunately the strike was not really general. Instead the T. U. C. wished it to be known as the National Strike instead of the old Syndicalist name. The General Council, apparently on the initiative of Bevin, decided to divide the workers' forces into two sections, front line and reserves. The front line, composed of the printing trades, railmen, busmen, tramwaymen and other road transport workers and dockers, were called out from midnight, May 3. The reserve line of engineering and shipyard workers, iron and steel and chemical workers, the textile industry and the building trade were not called out until the last day of the strike, *after it had been called off*. This division of the workers' forces is a particularly stupid example of the attempted application of military rules to a social conflict.

The result of the division was to isolate the strikers in certain towns where they formed a minority. Let us consider the example of Coventry, a very compact town devoted entirely to engineering. Such a town does not depend on road transport proportionately as much as London does. Nor is Coventry a railway centre. So, in Coventry the strike was limited to the railmen, a small body of busmen and a few printers. The case of Coventry was repeated in hundreds of other towns given over to engineering, textiles and chemicals; the strikers were to be small bodies of trade-unionists separated from the mass of their fellows.

Fortunately the workers thought differently. Again we shall take the example of Coventry as being typical of the whole country. The workers of the Armstrong-Whitworth Aircraft Company trudged gloomily from Coventry to the aerodrome on Whitley Common. Arriving there they found the hangars surrounded by the military. The first arrivals refused to enter while the place was under military control and when their numbers increased a decision to join the strike was made. Returning to Coventry the strikers besieged the district offices of the Amalgamated Engineering Union and sent small parties to the auto factories to inform their fellow engineers. The aircraft workers successfully demanded a district aggregate meeting of A. E. U. members and the meeting decided to close the engineering shops of the city on May 6. Much the same was happening in many parts of the country. The workers were making the strike general.

Nor were the workers content to spread the strike - they had to make it effective. Immediately they turned their attention to transport picketing. The stoppage of road and rail transport was almost complete the first day. In London only 40 of the 5,000 buses ran; in most towns no attempt was made to run tram or bus services throughout the strike. But quickly the student and middle-class blacklegs appeared on the roads, mainly to drive lorries.

Class Against Class

The almost instinctive strategy of the masses was superior to that of their self-esteemed leaders. The workers knew that a modern state depends on centralisation and concentration of power and that centralised power could be effective only by the use of intricate communications, electric power, telephones and telegraphy, railways and road transport. So the strikers and the unemployed formed themselves into mass road and rail pickets.

The road pickets were particularly effective in the mining areas for the miners did not need to picket their blackleg-proof pits. No student ever went down a mine to scab on a miner; they preferred sitting in the driver's seat of a car, with a big policeman each side to stop the bricks. A glance at the map will remind us that the chief communications arteries of England run north to south and near the Border are narrowed down by the waist of Britain and the Pennine Chain, so that the two slim sets of railways and roads skirt the east and west coast. One of these, the east, runs through the Northumberland and Durham coalfields, and there took place the most effective picketing of the strike.

Throughout the country buses and lorries were overturned and often petrol bowsers were fired. In some towns huge car parks were formed of blacklegs' vehicles and their drivers were often taken prisoner. On the railways a scattered warfare was carried on and the B. B. C. and 'press' reported damage to points, blackleg platelayers running for their lives,

24

telegraph wires cut and signal boxes successfully attacked. The Flying Scotsman express was derailed by miners at Cramlington, Northumberland. The B. B. C. gave a stirring account of the workers' attack on the central railway station at Middlesbrough. At 9 p. m. on Thursday, May 6, the workers stopped a train at a main live crossing in the middle of the town and then in one spirited charge captured the station and blocked the line with heavy wagons.

We must not suppose that the General Council had the slightest sympathy with such robust action. At the beginning they had urged the workers to stay at home or play games. They even suggested that the workers play football with the police. The miners had ideas how a football match with the police should be run. Such ideas are not approved by the Football Association.

Revolutionary Beginnings

The mass pickets gave enormous strength to the transport permit committees. These committees had been formed when the Government refused the T. U. C. offer to carry on food transport along with the health services. The purpose of the committees was to check the claims of, and grant permits to, those wishing to transport food or other essentials. In most localities employers ignored the Government transport committees and humbly presented their claims to the strikers' permit committees. In Northumberland and Durham the O. M. S. broke down and the Government's Regional Commissioner at Newcastle pleaded to the Joint Strike Committee to join him in dual control of the food distribution.

The attack on other forms of communication was gravely hindered by the timidity of the General Council. Post Office, telephone and telegraph workers were never called out. The position of the electricity supply workers was very obscure. The General Council talked of cutting off power but maintaining light. In most cases the electrical workers settled the problem by coming out.

While the workers struck at the communications of the enemy, they at the same time organised their own. Thousands of cars and motorcycles, tens of thousands of cycles stood ready at strike headquarters or sped along the roads, the black and yellow T. U. C. label clearing the road before them.

The strike was organised in each town by a hastily formed Council of Action. In some cases these councils were just the old trades councils or their executive committees. In other cases entirely new councils were formed by delegates or officials from district offices of the chief unions. In Northumberland and Durham the local Councils of Action were federated into a regional council covering the important industrial area of the North East, controlling the two coalfields and the ports and shipyards of the Tyne, Tees and Wear, with the great engineering and chemical works and the north-south traffic routes.

The councils suffered a great deal from lack of daily contact with the masses of strikers and most of the stirring and really effective actions were unorganised and spontaneous.

The Government's chief weapons were a great display of military force, police terrorism and heavy propaganda. Attempts to run the economy of the country were secondary to these. No newspapers appeared (though most newspaper offices published a few duplicated bulletins) until the Government issued the *British Gazette*. Churchill was chief editor. The paper was published at a great loss. In Durham it was distributed by dropping copies from aircraft, a method reminiscent of war. In most localities copies were slipped into the letter-boxes of working-class homes at night. The B. B. C., however, was the Government's chief propaganda weapon.

The T. U. C. could have overcome any effects of the B. B. C. by holding a thousand or so meetings every day. Those were the days of open-air Labour propaganda and crowds would quickly have assembled. Instead, the General Council discouraged meetings. 'In common with my principal colleagues, I avoided speechmaking and advised against mass-meetings of strikers or sympathisers.' (*Memoirs*, Clynes.)

Printed propaganda for the strike had been prohibited by the T. U. C. ban on all printing, even the T. U. C.'s own *Daily Herald* coming under the ban. Local strike committees got round the ban by issuing cyclostyled bulletins. After a few days the General Council issued the *British Worker* in reply to Churchill's *British Gazette*.

In the House of Commons Sir John Simon, speaking as a lawyer declared the General Strike to be illegal. Much has been made of this since, but at the time it did not have the slightest effect on the strikers. The Government did not limit itself to propaganda. In the Clyde, the *Hood* (then the world's largest battleship), the *Warspite* and the *Comus* threatened the working-class quarters with their guns. Destroyers lay in the harbours of Harwich, Cardiff, Portsmouth and Middlesbrough. The London power stations were manned by naval engine-room ratings and naval men worked in the London docks. A submarine supplied electric power to the Port of London.

The London docks were besieged by striking dockers and middle-class blacklegs were afraid to go there. The docks were heavily guarded by soldiers in full war kit and machine guns were mounted everywhere. The Home Secretary met high army and naval officers. 'Make your plans, he said. Use whatever force you require - I give you carte blanche - but

26

my orders are that the London docks must be opened at all costs.'

Warships took loads of blacklegs down the Thames at night and one hundred food lorries were loaded. Next morning the lorries passed through the East End in convoy, guarded by hundreds of police, two battalions of infantry with fixed bayonets, a number of tanks and ten armoured cars.

Every day the strike became more clearly a struggle between two classes, a fight between the workers and the State. The struggle itself created that clear picture. It was not a result of propaganda, as the Labour leaders wailed.

The whole crux of the struggle had been skilfully shifted by propaganda from a sympathetic protest at the unfair treatment of the miners to a Constitutional struggle between Parliament and Anarchism. (*Memoirs*, Clynes.)

Betrayed

As the strike developed, more workers joined it, the picket lines increased, the tourniquet on the high roads tightened. There was never any slackening of the strike. According to Professor W. H. Crook (*The General Strike* pp.390-396) quoting reports of the Ministry of Transport, 99 per cent of London Underground workers struck. On the Great Western Railway by May 11 only 8.4 per cent of goods trains ran; on the London Midland Service less than 3 per cent and on the London & North Eastern Railway less than 1 per cent. Railwaymen claim that these figures were exaggerated by running the trains over much shorter distances and so increasing the number of trains, but not the goods carried.

The reply of the Government was to increase the terror. The limits of their own laws were too narrow for them. Thrusting aside the Constitution and laws, the Cabinet, no doubt with memories of their Black and Tans, promised immunity to the Forces for any violence they might wish to commit. On May 7 they broadcast this announcement:

'All ranks of the Armed Forces of the Crown are hereby notified that any action which they may find it necessary to take in an honest endeavour to aid the Civil Power will receive, both now and afterwards, the full support of His Majesty's Government.'

Nevertheless, the Armed Forces were little used other than as a threatening parade. The chief forces of the Government were the regular police, the Special Constabulary and an extra special body of mounted 'specials' recruited from the well-to-do to form Cossack troops. Their chief weapons were wholesale arrests, where the strikers were not too strong, and wild baton charges, often on crowds coming out of theatres and cinemas. But the strikers stood firm. The two classes confronted one another, as over a barricade.

As the strike developed some members of the ruling class, particularly those running municipalities, showed signs of worry. The Newcastle City Council, with a heavy Conservative majority, called upon the Government to seek an armistice. The Archbishop of Canterbury, after consulting the leaders of the churches, appealed for the calling off of the strike, the withdrawal of the miners' lock-out and the renewal of the coal subsidy until a settlement was found. The anxiety was not limited to City Councillors and parsons.

'J. H. Thomas, representing the railwaymen, found, early in the Strike, that his duties took him to Buckingham Palace. King George asked him a number of questions and expressed his sympathy for the miners. At the end of the talk, His Majesty, who was gravely disturbed, remarked, it is said: 'Well, Thomas, if the worst happens, I suppose all this - (with a gesture indicating his surroundings) - will vanish?'

Fortunately for Britain and the world, it did not come to the worst. The Trades Unions saw to that.' (*Memoirs,* Clynes.)

Thirty Pieces

But the Government was undisturbed; it knew its agents in the Trade Union movement. All during the Strike the General Council was seeking anything which looked like a way out. In the course of their seeking they met Sir Abe Bailey and Sir Herbert Samuel at the former's house. Samuel proposed terms of settlement which included wage cuts and some vague re-organisation of the mining industry. That was sufficient for the General Council who pretended that the proposals were, somehow, coming from the Government. Sir Herbert Samuel was quite clear about this, saying: 'I have been acting entirely on my own initiative, have received no authority from the Government and can give no assurances on their behalf.'

The Government, through the Minister of Labour, Sir Arthur Steel-Maitland, declared that no terms would be considered, or negotiations opened, the strikers must surrender unconditionally.

Returning to the miners' leaders the General Council presented these unofficial and private conversations as terms of settlement, speaking airily of guarantees.

'Mr. Pugh was continually pressed and questioned by Mr. Smith (the M. F. G. B. president), myself and my colleagues as to what the guarantees mentioned were and who had given them. We got no answer.' (A. J. Cook, *The Nine Days*).

The miners' leaders contemptuously rejected the shufflings of the General Council and expressed their determination to carry on the fight. The Council deputation then went to 10 Downing Street and Pugh, addressing Baldwin, said:

'We are here today, sir, to say that this General Strike is to be terminated forthwith in order that negotiations may proceed.' (Wednesday, May 12, 1926).

Once again workers looked at one another with bitter eyes and said 'We are betrayed!'

Immediately the police terror was renewed. The number of arrests increased after the strike and baton charges continued. On the night of Wednesday, May 12 a meeting of dockers was being held outside Poplar Town Hall when a lorry full of police drove through the crowd, scattering injured people to each side. Father Groser, the vicar, held up a crucifix and told the police the meeting was peaceful. He, too, was batoned. The same night a van-load of police was driven to the headquarters of the Poplar branch of the National Union of Railwaymen. Without warning the police charged into the building and batoned all within reach.

When the strikers returned to their places of work the following day, hundreds of thousands of them were met by victimisation, demands for non-unionism, wage reductions or dismissals. The railwaymen were the chief victims and spontaneously renewed the strike. The threat of a new General Strike, without the leaders, curbed the viciousness of the employers' attack, yet even then thousands of men were victimised. In sullen anger the workers returned and the miners were left to fight alone until November when, driven by hunger, they accepted defeat. Wages were cut, the working day was increased from seven to eight hours and district agreements replaced the national agreement.

Post Mortem

It is now our task to examine the various social bodies and forces at work in the Strike and from a study of their relationship find lessons valuable to the workers in their struggle against the employing class. *The Government and the Employers -*' The old revolutionary statement that the State is but the executive committee of the ruling class' was well justified by the events of 1926. From the beginning to the end of the struggle the 'Constitution' was on the side of the mine-owners. All the old social-democratic nonsense of the State being above classes was cruelly pushed to one side by the employers and their government. Although the *Conservative Party was* in power, the *Liberal Party* was whole-heartedly behind the coalowners. In times of strike the Popular Front sham of

29

'progressive' Liberalism is flung aside and the Liberal coalowner is at one with his Tory brother. The Popular Front can wait until the next General Election.

A fairly large *Fascist* movement existed in 1926 in the form of the British Fascisti. Forgotten were the 'social' message and 'workers' charter' of Fascism. The Fascists joined the O. M. S. and drove lorries or unloaded ships, as did the other blacklegs.

The role of the leaders of the *T. U. C.* and the *Labour Party* was particularly despicable for they had always been opposed to the General Strike and never at any time had they withdrawn their opposition to it. By leading a struggle they opposed, they took the part of agents-provocateurs. It seems that the Labour leaders believed that a struggle in defence of the miners was inevitable and that it was better to initiate the fight in order to control and hamstring it. In any case, what treachery lacked, cowardice made up.

'It must not be forgotten that apart from the rights and wrongs of calling a General Strike, there would in any case, with the miners' lockout, have been widespread unofficial fighting in all parts of the country, which would have produced anarchy in the movement.' (Ernest Bevin in *The Record.*)

'What I dreaded about this strike more than anything else was this: if by any chance it should have got out of the hands of those who would be able to exercise some control, every sane man knows what would have happened. I thank God it never did.' (J. H. Thomas in the House of Commons, May 13, 1926.)

'Every day that the strike proceeded the control and the authority of that dispute was passing out of the hands of responsible Executives into the hands of men who had no authority, no control, and was wrecking the movement.' (Charles Dukes, N. U. G. & M. W., Report 1927 Conference of Executives.)

'I have never disguised that in a challenge to the Constitution, God help us unless the Constitution won.' (J. H. Thomas, House of Commons, May 3, 1926.)

'I have never favoured the principle of a General Strike.' (J .H. Thomas at Hammersmith, May 9, 1926.)

'No General Strike was ever planned or seriously contemplated as an act of Trade Union policy. I told my own union in April, that such a strike would be a national disaster. . . .We were against the stoppage, not in favour of it.' (*Memoirs,* Clynes.)

The *Independent Labour Party* was at that time anything but independent and was still affiliated to the Labour Party, a majority of Labour Members of Parliament and ex-Cabinet ministers being members of the I. L. P. The attitude of the I. L. P. was essentially that of the Labour Party; its leaders, Snowden and MacDonald, had years before opposed the General Strike in their long disputes with the Syndicalists. In 1926 MacDonald was still leader of the I. L. P., as well as the Labour Party, and was still repeating his old opposition to the General Strike.

'I don't like General Strikes. . . .I am terribly cold-blooded about the matter. . . .With discussion of General Strikes and Bolshevism and all that sort of thing I have nothing to do at all.' (Ramsey MacDonald, House of Commons, May 3, 1926.)

The *Communist Party* had never yet aspired to being anything more than the vague left wing of the Labour Party and trade unions. The crises of 1925 and 1926 found them without any alternative policy to that of the labour leaders. On the second day of the Strike the Communist Party issued a manifesto repeating the M. F. G. B. slogan 'Not a penny off the pay, not a minute on the day' and adding a self-contradictory call to 'Nationalise the Mines under Workers' Control without Compensation' and the formation of a Labour Government. That is a Government of MacDonald, Snowden, Clynes and Thomas! The miners must wait until the next General Election for that! To these slogans the Communist Party added the one it had used since the beginning of the crisis - 'All power to the General Council.' A stupid parody of the slogan of the October Revolution 'All power to the Soviets.' 'All power' to Thomas, Clynes and Bevin. They already had too much power - the power to betray the miners.

There existed at this time a trade union opposition known as the *Minority Movement,* a thinly disguised Communist body. Shortly before the strike, in the usual Communist fashion, it claimed to have an affiliated membership of 1,000,000. Being a Communist organisation it was forced to trail behind the C. P. and during the Strike, in which it played no part, it even ceased to hold meetings. A few years later it perished miserably.

We Shall Rise Again

No *Syndicalist* movement existed in Britain in 1926, although until the end of the Great War a small propaganda movement had lived vigorously. Unfortunately this movement had been eclipsed by the Russian Revolution or engulfed by trade union work. Nevertheless the General Strike propaganda of the old Syndicalist groups had had a much greater effect than was ever expected of it. The idea of the General Strike appealed to the imagination and conscience of the British worker.

The present Syndicalist movement in England was as yet unborn in 1926. The betrayals of a decade, the failure of two Labour Governments,

31

the Labour desertion of the Spanish Revolution and the Socialist-Communist support of the second world war were to later make inevitable the creation of our present Revolutionary Movement.

Without a Syndicalist minority among the miners, factory workers and transport men, on the picket lines and at local strike headquarters, the strikers were easy prey to the Judas Iscariots. Without such a strong, compact and resolute body of conscious revolutionaries, no alternative to the treacherous leadership could be found.

Of the workers, nothing but the highest praise is sufficient. They responded to the strike call magnificently. When the Government wished to publish the *British Gazette* not one linotype operator could be found to set up its paper. In thousands of cases trade unionists walked out to certain dismissal. In many cases, especially on the railways, men in supervisory posts sacrificed jobs and pensions to join the fight. The ninth day of the strike found the workers more determined than ever to carry on the fight. There was never any drift back. What the workers lacked was revolutionary understanding and organisation. It is our task to create these. The General Strike is not dead. Weighing carefully the treachery and cowardice of labour leaders and drawing inspiration from the courage and sacrifice of the workers, we prepare ourselves for the Second British General Strike.

Principles of Syndicalism

Principles of Syndicalism 1

Not Centralism - But Federalism

The striking worker, once he ceases work, must face such problems as, 'How shall we pay the rent, how buy groceries, how renew the kiddies' shoes?' Is it not then natural that he should look to his union for the payment of a little strike benefit? He has paid, perhaps, two shillings a week for ten, fifteen or twenty years and drawn out not a penny. He has been told by his leaders that the union's funds add up to five or six million pounds. They told him that it was wise to pay his union dues to meet such a need as this.

Unhappy man, to expect anything back from the clutching hands of bureaucrats. First of all he will find that the strike is termed unofficial (more than 99 per cent of strikes are 'unofficial', in peace as in war). It may be in defence of some trade union agreement, it is probably in defence of wages, it will most certainly be just that case for which the worker has paid his trade union contributions. Nevertheless, down to the district or factory will come the trade union officials to condemn the strike.

First will come a lesser bureaucrat. 'Lads, I sympathise with you. You are right, but I have my duty to do. You must go back to work!' Next comes the big boss. He does not waste time on euphemisms or good manners. The strikers are a bunch of scoundrels led by agitators and Anarchists, he hints darkly that if they don't go back to work he will call the police and in any case they won't get any strike pay so they will be starved back.

Does it not occur to the striker to ask 'Who is this person to say I must go back to work? Why should he have the power to withhold from me my own money?' Yes, it does occur, but the worker has long been trained in the centralist principles of trade unionism and the state. (Trade unions are organised on the same highly centralised principles as is the capitalist state.)

The trade unionist is in a dilemma. He knows that the strikers, assembled at their place of work, are the ones to decide when to strike, when to pay benefits and what shall be official and what unofficial. But, nevertheless, he wishes the workers' organisations to be so linked that they present one solid, nation-wide front against the common enemy. He does not wish to see the labour forces split into a thousand small units to

33

be tackled one at a time by the boss, and, too often, he believes that centralism is the only way of achieving this. We affirm that there is another way and deny that centralisation achieves its claimed objective.

Centralisation takes control too far away from the place of struggle to be effective on the workers' side in that fight. Most disputes arise in the factory, bus garage or mine. According to trade union procedure the dispute must be reported to the district office of the union, (and in some cases to an area office) then to head office, then back again, then the complicated 'machinery for avoiding disputes' devised by trade union leaders and the employers' lawyers is set in its ball passing motion, until everyone forgets the original cause of all this passing up and down. The worker is not allowed any direct approach to, or control of the problem. We are reminded of the memoirs of a certain court photographer who was making a picture of the old Emperor of Austria to turn his head a little to the laft. Of course he could not speak to an emperor, so he put his request to a captain of the court guard, who spoke to his colonel, who spoke to a count, the count passed the request to a duke and he had a word with an archduke who begged his Imperial Majesty to turn his head a little to the left. The old chap turned his head and said 'Is that sufficient?' and the message trickled back to the photographer via archduke, duke, count, colonel and captain. The humble thanks travelled back by the same road. The steps of trade union communication are just so fixed.

Centralisation does not bring that class solidarity which the worker seeks. Decades of experience support us in this statement. The miners' defeat of 1921, the betrayal of the General Strike of 1926 and the course of every strike since the last world war are evidence of this. Trade union machinists have blacklegged officially, on striking iron moulders, engineers on boiler-makers. Trade union transport workers have carried blacklegs to mine and factory. The National Union of Railwaymen have scabbed on the Society of Enginemen and Firemen. In every dispute, for one striker there are a score of trade unionists to supply the strikebreakers with power, transport, light, heat, communications and all the many means without which modern industry cannot exist.

Even when the men concerned are members of one union blacklegging still goes on. The London busmens' strike of 1937 was broken by the continuance at work of the trolley-bus and tramwaymen, members of the same Transport and General Workers' Union as the petrol busmen who obeyed Bevin's orders to remain at work. Had the transport workers obeyed their own class loyalty, had they controlled their own affairs, who can doubt that they would have struck in solidarity with their fellow workers.

In contrast to this official trade union blacklegging we have the class solidarity of the Swedish revolutionary unions spoken of by Jim Connolly in his pamphlet *Socialism Made Easy.* Connolly in turn is quoting the *New York Sun.*

'If the offending business man happens to be a retail merchant, all workmen are warned off his premises. The drivers for the wholesale houses refuse to deliver goods at his store; the truckmen refuse to cart anything to or from his place, and so on; in fact he is a doomed man unless he comes to terms with his union. It is worth mentioning that boycotting bulletins and also names and addresses of those who are bold enough to help the man are published in leading type in all the Socialistic newspapers. . . .

'If the boycotted person be a wholesale dealer the proceedings are much the same, or rather they are reversed. The retailers are threatened with the loss of the workmens' trade unless they cease dealing with such a firm; the truckmen refuse to haul for it. It has even happened that the scavengers have refused to remove the refuse from the premises. More often, however, the cans are 'accidentally' dropped on the stairs.'

How are we to achieve rank-and-file control of the unions and yet gain the maximum co-ordination of the labour forces? Syndicalism solves the problem in a simple and straightforward way.

The basis of the Syndicate is the mass meeting of workers assembled at their place of work, factory, garage, ship, loco shed or mine. The meeting elects its factory committee and delegates. The factory Syndicate is federated to all other such committees in the locality - textile, shop assistants, dockers, busmen and so on. In the other direction the factory, let us say engineering factory, is affiliated to the District Federation of Engineers. In turn the District Federation is affiliated to the National Federation of Engineers.

Such federations are formed in each of the twenty-five to thirty industries and services - Rail Federation, Transport Federation and so on. Then, each industrial federation is affiliated to the National Federation of Labour, the co-ordination of all the workers' forces.

But how the members of such committees are elected is most important. They are, first of all, not representatives like Members of Parliament who air their own views; they are delegates who carry the message of the workers who elect them. They do not tell the workers what the 'official' policy is; the workers tell them.

Delegates are subject to instant recall by the persons who elected them. None may sit for longer than two successive years, and four years must elapse before his next nomination. Very few will receive wages as delegates, and then only the district rate of wages for the industry. We want none of the thousand a year fat trade union bosses.

35

It will be seen that in the Syndicate the members control the organisation - not the bureaucrats controlling the members. In a trade union the higher up the pyramid a man is the more power he wields; in a Syndicate the higher he is the less power he has.

The factory Syndicate has full autonomy over its own affairs. The district deals only with the general conditions of the district and industry; the national with those things which are general nationally but not particular to the primary Syndicate.

By such an organisation the workers would be able to express in deeds their solidarity with striking fellow-workers. The only hope of the greatest labour force being turned onto any dispute is that feeling of class solidarity. It is for us to allow it organisational expression,

'An injury to one is the concern of all.'

Principles of Syndicalism 2

Economic Federalism

In the first article in this series published in the previous issue of War Commentary we outlined the Syndicalist organisation. First the assembly of workers and their job committee at their place of employment, factory, ship, mine, shop, office, etc. Next the federation of factory or job committees of each one industry into a district industrial federation, as the Scottish Miners' Federation, the Yorkshire Textile Federation, the Midlands Railmens' Federation and so on for each industry and each economic district. From these come the national federation of each industry, road transport, engineering, distribution, building, etc. Then all national industrial unions or syndicates are federated to the National Federation of Labour covering the whole economy of the country. In the other direction, each factory meeting and committee is affiliated to the local council of syndicates, somewhat like the familiar Councils of Action, though much more thorough.

In our first article we applied the Syndicalist principle of organisation to the present stage of the class struggle alone. But the same principle is applied during the Revolution when the class struggle bursts its normal bonds of social restraint and the two classes confront one another over the barricades.

The factory, pit and other job organisations take possession of the places of work and operate them for the working class and cut off the

36

supplies and services of the employing class. The millers supply the flour to the bakers, the bakers distribute bread to the people. The power station workers send electric current to the factories while receiving coal from the revolutionary miners. The Farm Workers' Syndicate collects food and sends it to the towns; the Municipal Workers' Syndicate maintains the essential services of town life and communications are re-established by the postal workers. Rail, road and water transport workers carry goods and services among the many industries and localities.

At the same time the grip of the Syndicates upon the social economy prevents the employing class obtaining the essentials of existence. No food, no water, no gas, no servant for their homes. The more time they spend cooking or carrying buckets of water the less time they have for blacklegging or shooting workers. No trains, no petrol for their cars, no ammunition from the factories, no telephone, no newspaper to print their obscene lies.

Other tasks are carried out by the various organs of the syndicates, chief of these is the extension and defence of the revolution. The raising and arming of the Workers' Militia is chiefly the work of the factory committees and the organisation of Workers' Patrols to guard against hooligans and counter-revolutionists is that of the local Council of Syndicates. Without goods and services to be bought, the cheque books of the capitalists become useless; they can no longer hire the services of thugs and blacklegs.

With the triumph of the Revolution the functions of the Syndicates change and develop, but the constructional principle remains the same. The purpose of the committees and federations is now solely that of running the social economy, the industries and services. What men consume no longer depends on how much money each possesses or on the oscillations of the market, but upon on what men need and the capacity of industry to meet those needs.

The National Federation of Labour will meet quarterly, monthly, or at whatever intervals are found necessary, to consider the economic programme. Guided by the trends in taste, the rise and fall of particular demands and information supplied by the Distributive Workers' Syndicate they will form the programme of each group of utilities. If 200,000,000 yards of wool textiles are likely to be needed for the coming year, then that task will be handed to the Textile Workers' Syndicate who will divide the task among their districts. In turn each district will allot the share of the district task to each mill, according to the number of workers and the machine capacity of the undertaking.

To the Clothing Workers' Syndicate will be given the work of producing so many suits, coats, etc. To the Miners' Syndicate the responsibility to raise so much coal, the Iron and Steel Syndicate so much finished metal, the Wood Workers' Syndicate so many articles of furniture.

Through the same channels will be expressed the needs of the Syndicates as well as the needs of individuals. The Iron and Steel Syndicate requires ore, limestone and coke. The Construction Syndicate needs timber, bricks and cement. The economic council of labour makes possible complete economic planning instead of the present chaos. It is not Syndicalism which means chaos; it is the present capitalist system which has brought society to the greatest chaos, economic and political, ever known.

The considerations of the national economic council will not, of course, be limited to one particular country. While each country and region will develop its own resources, as against the ways of international finance capital, there will remain many utitlities which can better be made, or grown, in certain areas. It will be the work of the economic council to import such things, say oranges to Britain, and to export others, say textile goods or machinery.

Let us here correct a misconception which may be creeping into the minds of some readers. Syndicalism is not nationalistic. The international character of Syndicalism has found expression in the International Working Mens' Association, but historical conditions force us to fight within national boundaries and we do not determine the character of the class struggle. Nevertheless, Syndicalism seeks the complete abolition of national frontiers. Indeed, this must be the outcome of technological development if allowed to continue.

The political organisation of society, that is the government of men by men according to territory, must give way to a social organisation based on the administration of things, men regulating machines and utilities in a world economy.

The greatest tragedy of Europe is that complete economic districts are torn apart by frontiers which have no basis in science or nature. In the Mid-Rhineland the iron ore is on the French side of the frontier and most of the coal, coke ovens and power is on the German side, yet one is essential to the other. Throughout Europe frontiers cut through railways, rivers, canal systems and electric transmission to the impoverishment of the Continent and the fruition of war. Left to normal social development rivers unite men in communities. London stretches along along both banks of the Thames, Glasgow along the Clyde; the same is true of the Tyne, the Humber and the Mersey. But when men make frontiers they so often use rivers, not to unite, but to divide men. Rivers like the Rhine and the Danube, along whose banks great communities have grown, have been used as frontiers. Workers have been cut off from their employment and merchants from their trade. Families have been divided and towns ruined by the capricious boundary makers who call their crimes a peace conference.

The conflict of technics and politics threatens to make life impossible. Once one might say that Europe was one and stop at that; now one must say the world is one. Technics enable us to travel across the Continent in a few hours or encircle the Earth in a few days or send a message around its girdle in a few minutes. But politics works the opposite way. Even in peace time it took many days to travel across Europe, even with the most expensive mode of transport, because of the obstacles placed in one's path by political orgainisation.

Just before the last war, even with countries having a thorough passport system, few obstacles stood in the traveller's path. But just before the present war the barriers had grown enormously. To stricter passports were added visas, the customs were increased and an entirely new kind of money customs invented. As technology progressed, politics retrogressed. The final stage of the conflict of technics and politics comes when the latter, dividing men unto death, utilises the former for the construction of tanks, guns and planes to the destruction of the social economy.

It is the aim of Syndicalism to sweep away all frontiers, to untie humanity in a world federation of producers and end poverty, oppression, exploitation and war.

Principles of Syndicalism 3

Abolition of the Wages System

In this study of the wages system we are not concerned with some imaginary system which does not, has never, and is not likely to exist. Nor shall we discuss what would be the effect of the wages system if it were entirely different. We are content with the scientific method of observing what exists and from careful observation forming our generalisations. This is economics, not metaphysics, and economics ought to be objective. Primitive men seeing lightning and hearing thunder imagined them to be the signs of an angry God. The growth of scientific knowledge dispelled this view and enabled man to control this force.

We do not seek to explain economic manifestations by referring to good or bad employers or good or bad governments. We seek nothing less than the abolition of the wages system, for it is the system which is wrong. Without a knowledge of social economy we are as the savage facing natural forces. With knowledge of the subject we can control our social course.

What Is Wages?

We live in a commodity society where everything is made for sale. In other societies this was not the case. Savages and barbarians gathered or grew food for their own use and not for sale; built houses to shelter themselves and not to rent. Truly medieval society produced most things for consumption in the immediate locality, and even household, and sold only the surplus.

Capitalist society, however, produces everything for a market. The coalowner is interested in the production of coal, not for his own hearth, but to put upon the market. The mill-owner initiates the manufacture of cloth not, like those of old, because he needs a coat, but to sell the produce on the market. Everything in capitalism is for sale. Books and beer, coal and cosmetics, horses and haberdashery. And not only manufactured goods, but every human relationship is offered for sale - politicians and patriots, love and friendship, art and science, and (see Major Barbara) even the soul's salvation.

Thrust, at an unripe age, into this world market, the worker, the proletarian, the man without property, finds he can live only by selling and buying. But what has he to sell? Without patrimony, having no goods and lacking access to natural resources, he must sell the only thing left to him, his labour power, his ability to work. He sells his time, portions of his life. That part of his life which he hires to his employer, eight, nine or ten hours a day, is not his, he has sold that part of his life. And the price of this labour commodity is called wages.

How Are Wages Governed?

If we consider how the price of a commodity is arrived at we shall understand the nature of the wages system. In a free market the final factors in fixing prices are supply and demand. Of course there are substantial economic reasons for the existence of any supply or demand, but for the purpose of this article we shall be content to consider the final factors. We all know if a certain commodity is scarce and the demand is

40

great the price tends to rise sharply. If there is a glut of another commodity and a small demand (as herrings in the height of the season) the price will fall, if the free market exists.

Wages too, are so regulated in a free labour market. If labour is relatively scarce and jobs are plentiful, wages rise; but when depression comes and jobs are scarce and millions of unemployed seek jobs, then wages fall. The same principle applies to particular industries and jobs. A certain industry, as engineering in the twenties of this century, may have more workers than jobs; then wages fall in that industry. Another industry, as the building trade in the twenties, may have almost more jobs than workers; there, wages will, compared with other industries, rise.

The Vanishing Craftsman

Another example we shall take is that of the craftsman. Before the war of 1914-18 craftsmen received wages about double that of labourers. (Provincial engineering craftsmen received 37 to 39 shillings per week; their labourers 18 shillings per week). Now some persons believed the employer paid the craftsman double the labourer's wage because he admired his skill. Some even believed that he did it just to make the workers jealous of one another. The truth is that the employer could not hire men at less than the market price of 37 shillings per week. And if he paid more than he needed to he would soon cease to be a capitalist. A worker does not pay 10 shillings for an article whose market value is 5 shillings nor can he hope to obtain it for 2 shillings and 6 pence. Likewise the capitalist does not attempt to put himself out of business by defying the principles of economics.

The truth of the foregoing is testified to by economic tendencies during and after the last war. Engineering employers successfully sought to lessen the demand for craftsmen by creating semi-skilled and unskilled jobs through the further subdivision of labour, by developing the use of machinery and the use of war-time dilutees, and breaking down the old time apprenticeship custom.

At the same time the wages of many unskilled workers were creeping comparatively upwards by the slackening of the supply of cheap unskilled labour much of which had come from overseas, as Irish labour in the chemical and constructional industries and Polish labour in the Scottish mines and jute mills. Further, certain sections of unskilled labour combined to limit the supply of labour to their job, as the dockers. So the tendency of economic development has been to greatly lessen the 100% gap between skilled and unskilled labour. I have known highly skilled

41

craftsmen who threw up their engineering jobs at 1 shilling and 2 1/2 pence per hour to take employment as dockers at 1 shilling and 6 pence per hour. The development of the wages system has almost completely destroyed the craftsman myth.

Let us here generalise our views of the wages system by declaring that in a free market wages rise and fall with supply and demand. The worker may by strike action increase the one or lessen the other, but he cannot change the general tendency. During trade depressions the employing class allows the free labour market to operate, but during great labour booms, as in the present war, they seek to close the free market by the use of such measures as Bevin's Essential Works Order. Thus while the worker may, once or twice in his life enjoy a boom period, the general tendency of the wages system is to push him down to subsistence level; that is, to allow him little more than sufficient to fuel himself for the performance of his master's work and to raise more little wage slaves to replace him when he wears out.

Reforms and the Wages System

Rather than oppose the wages system reformists have proposed modifications and additions which leave the system substantially intact. The wages system mocks reforms. Let us consider a few examples of reforms which have but strengthened it. Free education has been on every Socialist reform list from Marx and Engels' Communist Manifesto to the latest Labour Party election programme. Such free education as the State supplies has benefited the employers, not the workers. More general elementary education has increased the supply of apprentices and shop assistants. Scholarship matriculation has produced cheap clerks and vacuum cleaner salesmen. Working-class access to university degrees has lowered the wages of thousands of technicians to that of general labour, as the Association of Scientific Workers so often testifies.

Pensions are another good old stand-by of the reform merchants. Some years ago the granting of 10 shillings per week pensions to State-insured men over 65 years of age was hailed as a great step to the millenium. But the worker of 65 could not live on 10 shillings a week, he must continue work and many employers quickly reduced the wages of such men by 10 shillings per week. It was useless to try to disguise one's age for the State issued special insurance cards to the 65's and over. The 10 shilling pension went to the employer, not to the worker. It was the same in the case of war pensions. From the end of the last war to the beginning of the present armament boom, one might read in any Labour

Exchange advertisements of jobs which ended 'For disabled ex-servicemen only' or 'Only men with disability pensions need apply.' It was not gratitude to the men who fought which led certain employers to insert such clauses in their wants. A glance at the wages offered soon convinced us that only a man with a pension could hope to live on such work. The employer was the true recipient of the ex-soldier's pension. We all know cases of ex-policemen retiring on pension and sharply competing for the jobs of public house managers and nightwatchmen.

One further example of the negation of reforms by the operation of the wages system. There have been many attempts to raise or pay wages by Acts of Parliament and Trade Boards, but the solid fact remains that in the trade and industries affected wages fall during depression as they do in uncontrolled industries. To prove this one could produce enough statistics to fill a hay wain.

The Machine and Wages

Not only reforms but other doubtful forms of progress fail to benefit the wage worker. New machinery, which by increasing production, ought to enrich the worker and lighten his toil serves only to enslave and impoverish him. Let us imagine the case of a factory owner who employs 100 men working on 100 machines. New machines which can produce twice as much are introduced so that 50 men may do the work previously performed by 100. In a saner society the 100 would cut their working hours by half or increase their income by 100%. Not so in this case. 50 workers are sacked and swell the ranks of the unemployed. The remaining 50 dare not demand a share of the increased productivity because of the threatened competition of the 50 unemployed. Indeed it often happens that the retained machinists are faced by a wages cut.

Is it not obvious that there is no hope of any substantial or permanent improvement of workers' conditions so long as the wages system exists?

Wages in the Fifteenth Century

Lest some of our readers are yet unconvinced, let us examine the progress of the wages system over the greater length of its existence. Bourgeois economists usually point to the period of 100 to 150 years ago and contrast it against to-day, crying, 'Look at the wonderful progress we have made.' They attempt to conceal the fact that at that period labour had sunk to its lowest economic level of more than

43

1,000 years. During the period in question modern British capitalism was getting into its full stride and in order to attain speedy supremacy reduced the workers and peasants to almost unbelievable depths. To get a true comparison of the progress of the wages system we must examine a longer period. Let us look back 500 years.

Professor Thorold Rogers, M.P. in the best standard work on the subject 'Six Centuries of Work and Wages' in illustrating the wages of the mid-fifteenth century takes as example a recorded building job at Oxford 1449 to 1450. The head mason was paid 4 shillings a week and the other masons 3 shillings 4 pence a week. What could be bought with the 4 shillings or 3 shillings 4 pence then? Thorold Rogers gives a list of average prices for those years.

Wheat 5 shillings 10 pence a quarter; oatmeal, 5 shillings; beef 5 shillings 1 penny the hundredweight; mutton 4 shillings 6 pence; pork, 5 shillings; geese 4 pence each; fowls, 1 1/2 pence each; pigeons 4 pence a dozen; candles, 1 shilling 1 penny the dozen pounds; cheese, one-third of a penny a pound; butter, 1/2 penny a pound; eggs, 5 3/4 pence for 120; firewood 1 shilling 10 1/4 pence the load; shirting, 6 pence a yard; and cloth 1 shilling 5 1/4 pence; Thus, a week's wages could purchase 112 pounds of beef, or 12 geese or 96 pounds of butter, and so on.

Rent, now the largest item in a worker's budget, often one third of his income, was in the fifteenth and earlier centuries, about a halfpenny or less per week. The peasant for 2 shillings a year rented a cottage and very large garden; he had also a share in the common pasture; he was able to keep poultry, pigs and a cow. He had the concession of collecting loppings and wind wood from the woods.

Rogers demonstrates that the working day then was of eight hours. 'The artisan who is demanding at this time an eight hours' day in the building trades is simply striving to recover what his ancestor worked by four or five centuries ago.' Nor was the work very hard or wearisome, for tired or hurried men cannot produce good workmanship.

Socialism and Wages

Almost alone among the movements claiming the support of the workers, Syndicalism opposes the wages system. While Marx oppposed the wages system, most of the parties calling themselves Marxist or Socialist support it . The Communist Party approves of it, and calls upon Marx to witness their orthodoxy, while in Soviet Russia the wages system has been extended, consolidated and become more extreme.

The Independent Labour Party has never advocated its abolition. On

44

the contrary the I.L.P. at one time advocated a 'Living Wage Policy' which they alternatively called 'Socialism in Our Time'. The Labour Party has never looked beyond nationalisation of certain industries on the Post Office model. Now, even that is modified to 'public utility corporations' on the lines of the London Passenger Transport Board, their own creation.

Syndicalism fights against the existence of the wages system, against a method of distribution based upon mens' market value and for a society based upon their needs and the infinite capacity of society to satisfy them.

Principles of Syndicalism 4

The End of the Money Trick

Two features of capitalism are essential to its existence - the wages system and a thorough and all reaching system of money relationships. Unfortunately men are now so used to living by money that they find it difficult to imagine life without it. Yet it should be obvious that no libertarian and equalitarian society could make use of money. Syndicalism, as well as ending the wages system, also aims at the destruction of money relationships.

Money, more than any other human product, has been the means of creating false values. We each know of persons who began by wanting money as the means to other ends, but who spent so much energy accumulating money they forgot their original aim and continued to live for money. For means become ends. Is it not obvious that the wealthy trade unions, which have collected hundreds of millions of pounds by the promise to pay strike and other benefits, are now capitalist investment trusts afraid of strikes which threaten their investments?

Socially too, money creates its illusions, giving a false notion of progress. We are always hearing of the great progress that is being made in the twentieth century, and the advance in workers' wages is often cited as example. Everyone knows, of course, that prices have advanced with, or before, wages. Yet, because the advance is gradual, such is the illusion of money, that few realise how small is the progress made.

A few days ago I listened to a conversation on soldiers' pay. All agreed that the private soldier of 1943 with his 2 shillings and 6 pence a day was immensely better off than the soldier of 1913 with his 1 shilling

45

a day. True, prices were higher, nevertheless 2 shillings and 6 pence is considerably more than 1 shilling. Let us see. The soldier spends his half-a-crown on small pleasures and refreshments. We shall compare the cost of these now and thirty years ago.

	1913	1943
Cigarettes (Woodbines) per 10	2d	10 1/2d
Matches, per dozen boxes	2d	1/6d
Beer, per pint	2d	11d
Cinemas and Music Halls		
(cheaper seats)	2d to 4d	1/- to 1/9d

As to snacks, always important to barrack fed soldiers, in 1913 these cost a few coppers a time. Now, nothing could be more impudent than the prices of indifferent meals so often served to service men, especially in the West End. And in 1913 public houses usually supplied free counter snacks of cheese, biscuits and pickles, and often beef sandwiches. No, the advance of the soldier's wage is just another example of the money illusion.

Money has developed out of all resemblance to that simple medium of exchange which our ancestors used to displace barter. Certainly it was more convenient than barter. But, whereas money once had a real economic value, a golden sovereign having twenty shillings worth of economic value, just as much as twenty shillings worth of shoes, now, money being paper and adulterated metal has no real value. Being economically worthless, it is potent as a deceiver of the workers, a source of illusions and false values, a hatcher of Beveridge plans.

Even at the paper money stage the monetary system does not halt its development. Now, big money transactions usually mean a new entry in another set of books. A big insurance company may subscribe ú100,000,000 to a War Weapons Week without a dime leaving the bank. Yet it is to this book-keeping trick that we are slaves. By such manipulation they can (and are now so doing) cause inflation and gobble up the savings of the petty middle class or the more fortunate workers. By this method they may, and do, reduce to a fraction the obligations of the insurance companies and gain control of smaller businesses.

The so-called War Debt is the greatest of all money tricks. There is no real wealth except that which is produced by labour applied to natural resources. Now every gun used, every bullet fired, every bomb dropped, has been paid for by human labour. One cannot borrow human labour from the future. In true economics there is no war debt. Yet, we owe thousands of millions for products of labour, and our descendants to the end of time must continue to pay usury on them. The harder we, the workers, toil producing planes and tanks and guns, the more money we owe as the price of these our products. It's a great trick.

The development of the money system has also led to that creation of modern imperialism, international finance capital, to the investment of capital abroad, and to the export of fluid capital, money, in the form of industrial loans. Putting it simply, an agent of certain industrialists goes to, say, a South American republic and points out to its rulers the country's need of a railway and his employers' fine products in that line. 'Yes,' reply the South Americans, 'We like your railways, but we have no money to buy one.' 'That's all right,' replies our super-commercial traveller, 'we'll find that for you.' A loan, with high discount and interest is floated on the London market and the South Americans buy the railways with borrowed money.

So far, so good, but interest has to be paid and, as the finance capitalist is not content, as we often are, with pieces of printed paper, goods are exported to Britain to cover the money bills. As most of the goods will be agricultural products it should be obvious that British agriculture must suffer to allow the foreign products of the international finance capitalist system to be dumped on the market. This has led to a strange corruption of public taste. Even in peace time I have seen country-women returning from town, with foreign machine-skimmed milk and margarine from West Africa in their baskets!

A little while ago I picked up the menu in a London restaurant and was delighted to find spiced ham on the list. To me that meant the hams cooked in delicate spices, once so well known in Northern England. Of course I ordered the delicacy, but lo and behold it was just our old friend Spam! Pickled, yes in obnoxious chemicals. Oh! the odium of being pickled in sodium.

Eggs, which were once those lovely white and gold things from shells, are now powder from a carton. Just as good as the real thing. Official, M. of F. In a few years time real eggs will be as strange to us as are bananas to war children and the taste of one will probably make us vomit. Still, exported capital and its system must have their return.

Great are the sacrifices that money demands. We have seen miners in Durham who, because they were out of work, shivered over the embers in their grates because they lacked the money to buy coal. Yet they sat above the richest seams in the country. We have seen textile and clothing workers in the West Riding without overcoats in winter because they had not the money to buy their own products. We know farm workers who have starved because unemployment meant they lacked the money to buy the food their labour might produce.

There is no economic wealth except that produced by labour applied to natural resources. Let the miners produce coal for their own and their fellows' use, let the textile workers produce cloth and the farm workers food for societies' needs without regard to money relations. Only thus can we conquer unemployment without going to war.

We know that it is hard for men who have always lived in a money society to imagine a life based upon natural principles, but consider, had we been born into different circumstances it would be just as difficult to imagine life with money. I suppose most of our readers saw the film Mutiny on the Bounty. They will recall a certain incident in the film. The mutineers having landed in Tahiti are welcomed by the natives who give them food, drink, and huts to live in. A pleasant life in return for a little labour. Christian, the rebel leader, wishing to show his gratitude gives the native chief a large coin, a piece of English money. The chief, puzzled, asks its purpose. Christian explains that in England all food is stored in shops and to obtain it one tenders money. 'And if you have no money?' asks the chief. 'Then you get no food,' replies Christian.

'What is wrong in England,' asks the old chief. 'Is there not plenty of fish, plenty of bread fruit, plenty of chickens?' 'Oh, yes,' replies the seaman, 'plenty of fish, plenty of bread fruit, plenty of chickens.' 'And if you have no money you starve?' returns the native. 'Yes, you starve,' is the reply. The old chief considers awhile, then shakes his head and says, 'I think I stay in Tahiti.'

Poor savage! Entirely without education of course.

Principles of Syndicalism 5

To Each According to his Needs

The rapid development of world capitalist production reached a critical stage at the end of 1929. In the first half of the thirties decade the machines were overflooding the warehouses with every kind of commodity, shoes, clothing, books, metals, timber, hides; newly launched ships were left to rust on the beach without a maiden voyage; stacks of food were burnt or piled for the rats to harvest. As the commodities accumulated factories closed and farms were abandoned; millions of men and women joined the unemployed queues. For the people did not possess sufficient money to buy back the goods they produced. It is futile to say, 'Why cannot the workers be given enough money to buy back the goods they produce?' for, as we demonstrated in a previous article, the wages system prevents the worker's income increasing with his productive power.

Given the capitalist system, there was only one way to employ the idle capital of the world. To turn it to war production; to producing shells and bombs instead of boots and food. To distribute them free to enemies and allies alike by dropping them on their cities. The other alternative was to end capitalist and state-socialist distribution and, continuing to make useful comodities, distribute them freely according to the needs of each. For the productive capacity of modern industry is such that everyone may have enough of the very best of food, clothing, housing, books and all the good things of life by the useful labour of each for a few hours a week. But it can never happen within the bonds of the wages and money systems.

The Syndicalist mode of distribution, then, causes the abolition of these systems and establishes the principle of 'to each according to his need.' Not according to the amount of money he has, or according to rank or birth, or according to strength or cunning, but according to need. There is more than enough for all, so why should any go short?

It is often asked (I cannot tell why) who shall determine the nature and limits of a person's needs? Obviously the person himself. If a number of us sit down to dinner at a common table, one may eat twice as much as the average person, another only half as much, but no one is troubled about this. It is left to each to judge the capacity of his own stomach.

So let it be with all utilities. One needs more food than another. One man has no child, another a few children, yet another, many children. Each will have greater or lesser needs than his fellows. Utilities must be free to all. Socialised production demands socialised consumption.

Every society has had some degrees of this mode of distribution. Primitive society a great deal, capitalist society very little. Nevertheless modern capitalist society does give us a glimpse of the principle of free access to goods and services. A hundred years ago many roads could only be travelled on payment of a toll, and some such still exist in England. But now most roads are free; each may travel them little or much, according to his own estimate of his needs. The same is true of bridges and even some ferries. We have public parks, museums and libraries. Is anyone upset if someone sits in the local park all day and every day, while another never enters it? Does a man worry that he never reads a book while his neighbour brings home two or three from the public library twice a week?

A partial application of the principle was made by introducing the penny post. Now it seems strange that a London letter to Edinburgh should have cost twice as much as a letter to York. Yet the proposal of the penny post raised a storm of protest. It was said that some would abuse it, for to many it seemed strange that a man writing from London to York should pay only as much for his stamp as one writing to Croydon. And to apply the principle to letters going as far even as Australia was to conservative persons just the last word in lunacy. Yet now, in postal matters, everyone approves of the principle of 'to each according to his needs.'

It is often said that if food were there to be taken some would eat too much. They might the first time, but I doubt if they would keep it up. Water is free, not in the sense that it is not paid for, that is gratis, but its personal consumption is unrestricted. Some drink about a pint a day each, a few several pints, while a few of my friends refuse to touch it, believing it to be a dangerous liquid which even rusts steel and rots shoes. Yet no one abuses the drinking of water. No one hoards it; accumulating buckets and barrels of it in garret and cellar. For each knows there is plenty for him when he needs it. If bread were free would our attitude to it be different? Would anyone try to eat half-a-dozen loaves a day?

It will be readily be seen that such a principle of distribution can only be applied when there is a sufficiency of production. If everyone's need of butter is 8 ounces a week and the stock available allows only of 4 ounces per head per week, then, obviously, another principle must be applied. While capitalist production is enormously high, most of it is designed for the manufacture of hardly useful, and even harmful, products. Until the Syndicalist productive organisation has brought order to the present chaotic industries, distribution must be equal between individuals. Of course, that does not mean that all will consume the exact amount of each particular commodity or utility, but that each shall have an equal share (choice of variety being left to each) of the aggregate of goods available for distribution.

In the case of certain goods being in very short supply the principle of rationing must be applied, but, let us make this clear, this case has nothing in common with the present system of rationing. The basic principle of the present government's rationing system is not the equal division of goods of which there is a natural shortage. There is no equality. If a person has a great deal of money he may buy whatever rationed goods he needs, even without breaking the law. On the other hand if a person be poor, and this is the case with hundreds of thousands of working people, he may be unable to buy his full ration, particularly of clothes.

Nor is the present rationing, in most cases, the result of shortage. It is an attempt to force the purchasing power of the people from the consumption of useful commodities to the production of munitions and governmental apparatus.

In the case of certain goods which are in very short supply, these would be reserved for those especially needing them. Black grapes were once associated with sick beds, but no invalid worker may now buy them

50

at the present price of 23 shillings a pound. Nevertheless stout and hearty bourgeois may eat them to surfeit.

While Syndicalism would divide equally the social income and ration equitably goods in shortage, the productive power would be immediately reorganised and set in motion to cure the shortage and then create such a plentiful supply of goods as to enable the social distribution to be accomplished.

Although we could not obtain at once the principle of 'to each according to his need' in all things, yet with some goods and services it would be possible to do this at once. The two principles we have outlined would, for a while, continue to exist side by side. The few cases of free distribution now existing would continue to exist and would be extended. All roads, bridges and ferries would be made free. Parks would be extended and multiplied and to them would be added the public access of moorland, mountain, stream and seashore. Public libraries would be increased and made into cheery, comfortable homes of books, instead of the ill-assorted collections of shabby volumes stored in mauseoleums they now are. The same principle of distribution would be extended to other goods and services, two or three, or even half-a-dozen at a time. Speaking personally, I believe the change would be much more rapid than most would dare to believe possible.

Cases for the early application of the principle of free distribution will readily occur to all of us. Postal service, travel and education are obvious examples. House rent is another. On the outbreak of revolution everyone will, naturally, cease paying rent. After the revolution it is unlikely that they will return to their former bad habit of sustaining the landlords.

It is often asked, 'but what if someone wanted a luxury steam yacht or a one hundred roomed mansion?' Well, such things are the product of social labour. At present a rich person may, by his use of money, force others to build him a steam yacht by keeping other employment from them. Under Syndicalism this would be impossible, and it is improbable that any greedy, selfish person would be able to kid a shipyard full of workers to build him a ship all for his own hoggish self. There would be steam luxury yachts, but they would be enjoyed in common. I apologise for introducing this question but it is a familiar friend at many of our meetings.

Whether you accept our view of distribution or wish to retain the present will depend on whether you are a 'practical' person or an idealist. If you are 'sane, level-headed and practical' you will want to live in poverty, dirt and ugliness. You will wear cotton suits and paper shoes; you will grow dyspeptic on a diet of cabbage and starch; you will work

51

yourself to death in a factory or allow your body to be used as common meat. All in order that you may destroy the homes and cities of your Continental neighbour, while he, moved by the same 'practical' principles, destroys yours.

But, if you are an 'idealist and a dreamer' you will object to living on a poverty standard in a world of plenty. You will choose to enjoy your full share of the good things of life. You will build cities instead of destroying them and heal and make happy your neighbours instead of maiming and killing them. You will play your part in the building of the New World which is not only possible but whose coming is imperative.

Principles of Syndicalism 6

Workers' Control of Distribution

In the present conditions of class struggle the Syndicalist distributive workers are organised on the same principles as the factory and other industrial workers. The basis and control of the organisation is in the meeting of the workers at their place of employment where their job committee is elected. Thus each large store would have a House Committee. In the case of smaller individual shops, as these are usually found in groups (as grocers, chemists, butchers, bakers, etc.) about cross-roads or minor thoroughfares, workers from each shop would meet to elect their group committee. Similarly the warehousemen in the wholesale trade would elect their warehouse committee.

As in the case of all other syndicates, the shop committees are federated to the local Federation of Syndicates, representing all Syndicalist workers in the locality. In the other direction, the Shop Committees are federated to the District Committee of Distributive Workers, and the District Committees to the National Council of Distributive Workers. The National Council is, like other syndicates, federated to the National Council of Labour, which brings together and co-ordinates the whole of the Syndicalist forces.

The work of the Distributive Syndicates is, of course, not only to wage a struggle for better working conditions and higher wages, but also to prepare for the taking over of distribution by the workers. To that end the Syndicalist shop and warehouse workers study

52

their trade. They observe and discuss where such and such commodities are stored and how they could be distributed more justly and with greater efficiency. This task is urgent, for workers must be fed during the General Strike and Revolution.

The Spanish Syndicalists acted in this way. The bakers of Barcelona, before the Revolution, knew the locality and amount of all stocks of flour, and the oven capacity of the city's bakeries. On the glorious 19th July, 1936, when the revolutionary workers of Barcelona went to the barricades, their baker comrades ensured them and their families bread. The Peasants' Syndicates co-operated with the Distributive Syndicates in the collection of food in the country and its distribution in the towns of Catalonia.

During the stay-in strike of the Italian engineering workers in 1920 the peasants' syndicates, the distributive and transport workers and the co-operatives combined to supply food to the strikers who held the factories for four weeks.

In Britain the workers of the mining areas, particularly Durham, have shown how they can feed the workers by collecting food and running communal kitchens during strikes of three, four, six months or even longer. The workers can and must ensure their own food supplies in strike and revolution.

The Revolution accomplished, the Distributive Workers' Syndicate will, of course, establish liaison with the productive syndicates most closely related to it; Farm Workers, Food Preparation Workers, Wood Workers, Textile Workers, Clothing Workers, Leather Workers, Printers and such.

It will be understood that the Syndicalist method of distribution, like the Syndicalist method of production, has nothing in common with the principles of political control advocated by most Socialists and even by most politicians of all brands in modern times. Political control means control first of all by Cabinet Ministers who usually have no experience of the technique they claim to direct. A country squire is made Minister of Mines, a lawyer Minister of Aircraft Production, a political journalist is made First Lord of the Admiralty. In municipal affairs, parsons, butchers and publicans pretend to run the trams, supervise education and manage the drainage system. Government by amateurs! Instruction by the uninstructed!

Distribution like industry is a thing of technics and requires direction by persons of experience, those who have given time and thought to the theory and practice of their craft. Distribution means more than standing behind a counter, handing over a packet of cigarettes and counting 3 pence change. Every shop assistant should be an expert at his job, and Syndicalism will give him the incentive to develop the interest which will make him an expert. A bookshop assistant should know something of literature and printing, a tailor's assistant something of clothes, and a provision hand something of food, its care and attractive presentation. They should be able to make the best of the goods and advise the customer.

Of course distribution involves much more thtan shop-keeping. Each centre of population has its warehouses while behind them are the special warehouses of the railway centres and docks. All these need a knowledge of certain technics. Meat refrigeration, banana ripening, ventilations of wood-ware and a thousand other problems require special knowledge and experience.

Examples of the disastrous effect of government interference in distribution are only too abundant. Resisting the temptation to choose too many of the hundreds of examples available, I pick one from the hat. Here are headlines from the Daily Express, 12th June, 1943:

TOMATOES ROT WHILE SHOPS GO WITHOUT

'In London yesterday shops complained that they had no tomatoes. In Manchester wholesalers complained that their tomatoes were rotting.'

It is left to the reader to supply further examples from his daily reading and, better still, his observation.

But, lest it is thought that all this is due to the difficulties of war-time, let us take examples from the first few months of war, when there was no air raid, no fighting on land, no labour shortage, and plentiful stocks of food abounded.

The following is taken from a pamphlet 'Chaos on the Home Front' published by the Co-operative Movement.

Scunthorpe Co-operative Society had a very successful creamery. 'We had a certain amount of good fresh butter in stock and on September 22, the Food Minister requisitioned it. The butter was kept there for a considerable time. Immediately they took it over they increased the price by 10 shillings a hundredweight, or £10 a ton. We were allowed to draw our own butter out of our own cooling chamber and pay the Food Ministry the increased price of 10 shillings a hundredweight.

The society had some butter they needed but were not allowed to touch. They wrote a letter to the Ministry saying that the butter was going bad and needed turning. The reply told them to send the butter to London, from there it went to South Wales. Was it fresh? The customers were.

'You used to get good sized prunes for 6 pence per pound. The Ministry requisitioned the whole lot and sold them back to the grocers at a price which means that the retailer cannot sell the big ones for less than 8 1/2 pence, or the small ones.

'But the outstanding example of official muddle was fish. On the outbreak of war the Ministry at once abandoned the East Coast ports and set up a fish distribution centre at Oxford, with a chain of branch centres. The scheme did not work, supplies failed to reach the places where they were wanted. Much fish went bad because of the length of time taken in unpacking it and repacking it.'

Experience of lecturing on the subject has brought to my notice doubts which exist in the minds of a few persons. Doubts which I would not otherwise have believed possible, for most of these problems, questions of human and trade relationships, have already been solved, even under capitalism.

The most frequent of these runs like this, 'But how will the wishes of the consumer be met? What organisation will the Syndicalists set up whereby the consumer may express his preferences?' No organisation, I hope. Such a special organisation is about the least likely way of his wishes being effectively expressed. Better the way developed by the people themselves.

Goods, as now, will be produced in great variety, for workers like producing different kinds, and new models, of goods. Now if some goods are unpopular, they will be left on the shelves to be devoured by mice and moths or embalmed by spiders. Of other goods more popular, the shops will be emptied. Surely it is obvious that the assistant will decrease his order of the unpopular line and increase his order of the popular. Every shop-keeper does that now and learns, often with uncanny accuracy, to anticipate his customers' need. Even the newspaper seller at the street corner must anticipate so many of News, so many of Star and so many of Standard; to balance himself between extra customers and left-over copies.

'But what if the productive syndicates refuse to meet the need of the consumers as relayed to them by the distributive workers?' cries our stubborn questioner, defending his last barricade. Well, it is something that just won't happen. Everyone who makes something wishes that thing to be useful and desirable. Man's work must have social meaning, must be useful, or he is unhappy in his work.

Some years ago it used to be said that one of the worst punishments of the military 'glasshouse' was for a man to fill a wheelbarrow with lead shot, push it to the top of an incline and then tip the barrow allowing the shot to roll back. He then descended and refilled the barrow, repeating the rest of the process. It was said that this meaningless task, like so many other military tasks, nearly drove the victims to madness. The lack of social meaning was the sting of the punishment, which must have been invented by a student of Dante.

Another 'problem' we have presented to us is that of someone wanting an article which is not in the shops and which is not made. But is this likely to happen? People are stimulated and guided in their choice of goods by what they see in the shops and catalogues. Is anyone likely to make a sketch of the peculiar footwear of the ancient Assyrians, take it to a shoe shop and say, 'Have you a pair of shoes like this, size six, please?'

All these are small problems which we can safely leave to the day when they arise. It is for us now to determine the general outlines of the New Society and lay its foundations. It is possible that the further stages will be much easier and more satisfying than we, in the dull, grey age of capitalism, had dared to hope.

Principles of Syndicalism 7

The Commune

In previous articles we have considered the vertical organisation of syndicates, from the factory or job committee to the district and national Council of Labour. We are now to consider the horizontal organisation, from the job committee to the local federation of syndicates.

The workers of each factory, mine, shop, garage, or other place of work in any one town or locality are affiliated to the local federation. Thus, any city, town, or group of villages may have an organisation representative of engineering workers, railmen, busmen, teachers, shop assistants, tailors, municipal workers, builders, clerks, musicians and other workers. Certain localities will have delegates from dockers, seamen, miners and textile workers according to local constitution.

However, besides the delegates of the industrial workers organised in syndicates at their places of work, there are delegates of other groups, the unemployed, housewives, and small groups of odd trades.

The syndicates will endeavour to retain the membership of workers who become unemployed, unlike the wealthy craft unions which consider an unemployed man a liability. An out-of-work member will be thought of as, say, an unemployed carpenter, instead of just 'one of the unemployed'. Where men are in and out of work continually this will not be difficult, but in 'normal' times of depression there are hundreds of thousands of men and women who lose all touch with their previous job

56

and organisation and fall back into the vast anonymous ranks of 'the Unemployed'. It is the task of Syndicalism to organise these men and women to fight against their miserable conditions, to prevent their being forced into blacklegging, and to become part of the forces of emancipation.

Where women are working in industry the syndicate organises them with the men, but millions of working women, particularly in certain parts of Britain, never return to industrial work or service after the day of marriage. Yet these women, who have no proper place in the orthodox organised labour movement, are at once a weakness and a great strength of the workers' movement. They are a weakness in a strike if they do not understand and appreciate the issues; they can slowly and steadily sap the will to victory of their struggling menfolk. But, if they understand the issues, they are a tremendous addition to our battle forces, as particularly the women of the mining areas have shown. They can organise food collections and communal kitchens, nursing service, entertainments and propaganda. They can carry out boycotts and strike picket lines. The industrial North has shown that women can do the latter job as well as men. Without doubt our Syndicalist movement must organise the housewife as well as the industrial woman worker.

As well as the factory committees, unemployed and housewives, the local federation of syndicates has to organise certain individuals and small groups who, because of the nature of their employment, cannot be organised in the syndicates of industry and service. Writers, artists, small dealers, odd job men and many others who have no syndicate will desire a part in the struggle. The local federation will organise them in local groups.

The chief task of the local federation in present circumstances is the mobilisation of all labour forces for strike action. In a rail strike they will ensure that busmen are not used against railmen. In a miners' strike they will see to it, that blackleg coal is not moved. The local forces of labour will be swung from sector to sector of the class front as the need arises.

As a centre of strike propaganda, particularly in the case of small, 'unofficial' strikes now so familiar to us, the local is invaluable. Almost every such strike is greatly weakened by lack of propaganda and information issued by the factory strike committee, which usually lacks the means of propaganda. With a well-organised local, any strike in a factory, shop, or mine will be immediately reported to that local. Supplied with all necessary facts the local operates its permanent propaganda and news service. Other jobs in the town and neighbouring locals are informed of the facts of the case. Public meetings are held and local bulletins issued. Unemployed and workers from other jobs swell the picket ranks.

But the strike activity of the local is not limited to propaganda. Collections must be made to augment the strike pay. Perhaps it may even be necessary to organise the collection or cheap mass purchase of food, or the formation of communal kitchens.

In the case of certain strikes the boycott is applied. In disputes of cinema or theatre workers, shop assistants, newspaper printers or the employees of firms selling branded goods, the boycott is an effective weapon.

The local form of Syndicalist organisation is not limited to cities and thickly populated industrial areas. The mining areas and the contryside also have their own type of local federation. In the country we usually find small villages grouped around a larger village or small country town. The same is true of the semi-rural semi-industrial mining areas. In these cases each village would have its sub-federation affiliated to the federation of the parent village, corresponding to the town federation.

It is natural that the delegates of the local will desire to establish contact with the delegates of neighbouring locals. To this end the local federation of syndicates in any region is affiliated to a regional confederation of labour, as Clydeside, the North East coast, Birmingham, South Wales or London. The Syndicalist mode of organisation is extremely elastic, therein is its chief strength, and the regional confederations can be formed, modified, added to or reformed according to local conditions and changing circumstances.

The opportunities of the local federation during the revolutionary struggle are too obvious to need underlining; organisation of workers' militia, propaganda, supplies and co-ordination of factory defence are the greatest of these.

With the triumph of the revolution and the passing of the class struggle the local organisation of Syndicalism changes character and becomes the Commune, an organisation of people who live together, for the purpose of living together. The Commune will take the place of the present unrepresentative borough council.

However, most of the functions of the municipalities will be carried out by the industrial syndicates. Local transport will be the responsibility of the Transport Syndicate, hospitals that of the Health Workers' Syndicate, education that of the Teachers' Syndicate, and so on. All of these services need men and women of experience, persons with some knowledge of the technical and intellectual problems, a knowledge not usually possessed by the typical town councillor. Local Education Committees, for instance, are usually bossed by elderly brewers, publicans, pork butchers, speculative builders, religious bigots and such like. Of course, the control of schools may be modified by the creation of teachers', parents', and scholars' councils, but such problems are a matter of experiment; we are now concerned with the creation of working class organisation which can take over education at once.

The abolition of the money basis of society will relieve the Commune of the chief task of the borough and county councils - the collection of rates. Nor will the Commune be concerned in running businesses, as many municipalities do, in order to gather profits to aid the rates.

The Commune, a much smaller and more intimate and decentralised body than the borough council, will be entirely devoted to improving the communal life of the locality. Making their requests to the appropriate Syndicates, Builders', Public Health, Transport or Power, the inhabitants of each Commune will be able to gain all reasonable living amenities, town planning, parks, play-grounds, trees in the streets, clinics, museums and art galleries. Giving, like the medieval city assembly, an opportunity for any interested person to take part in, and influence, his town's affairs and appearance, the Commune will be a very different body from the borough council, which is largely an organisation for the protection of the big ratepayers, hobbled and controlled by the Ministry of Health from Whitehall.

In ancient and mediaeval times cities and villages expressed the different characters of different localities and their inhabitants. In redstone, Portland or granite, in plaster or brick, in pitch of roof, arrangements of related buildings or pattern of slate and thatch each locality added to the interest of travellers. Scotland, the North of England, London, the West Country and East Anglia, each expressed itself in castle, home or cathedral.

How different is the dull, drab, or flashy ostentatious monotony of modern England. Each town the same. The same Woolworths', Odeon Cinemas, and multiple shops, the same 'council houses' or 'semi-detached villas', £50 down and 25 shillings and 6 pence for the rest of your life. North, South, East or West, what's the difference, where is the change?

With the Commune the ugliness and monotony of present town and country life will be swept away, and each locality and region, each person will be able to express the joy of living, by living together.

59

Principles of Syndicalism 8

Defending the Revolution

The Syndicalist objectives we have outlined in previous articles will not, of course, be carried out without arousing the fiercest opposition and most bitter hatred of the employing class. The expropriation of that class, the control of industry by the workers, the abolition of money and the wage system and the establishment of the principle of each according to his need can only be when we are prepared for the most revolutionary of struggles.

Our first weapon is the highest technical development of the principle of non-co-operation; cutting of economic supplies and services from the employing class and switching them to the workers; generally, refusing to do any work for or co-operate in any way in the observation of the laws and orders of the employers.

We do not need to be warned that the enemy will not, if our forces be weak enough, willingly accept this new condition. We know that he will if possible use against us the armed forces, the police and Fascist bands. But, acute social problems, particularly in the 20th century, sweep across the whole population including the armed forces. The Revolution will have as many adherents within the armed forces as it will have in the civil population.

Nevertheless the Revolution must be defended, by armed force if necessary, against those remnants of the armed forces the enemy may rally and against the Fascist militia, 'Black and Tans' or whatever they may call the new counter-revolutionist army they may raise.

To that threat the Syndicalist reply is the creation of the Workers' Militia. The chief base of the new workers' army will be the place of work, factory, garage, mill, pit or dock. There men know one another, know the man who is loyal to his class and he who might be a counter-revolutionist. Already a high degree of self and group discipline and of working and struggling together have been practiced. In the Spanish Civil War of 1936 the Workers' Militia was largely based on the squad of ten men known to one another and choosing their own squad leader or delegate. The squads of ten men were united into centurias of one hundred men and seven or eight centurias formed into a column, all on the federal principle.

The choice of the factory, etc., as the chief base of the Militia has an extra advantage in the present day warfare of highly mechanised forces. Thus, shipyard, dock and seamens' syndicates form naval units; bus and lorry drivers - transport and mechanised units; miners, bridge builders and construction workers - engineer battalions and so on. Not only is the skill and experience already assembled, but, also, the necessary machines are at hand to these units. Further, an industrial population can be trained much quicker than an agrarian populace in the use of weapons, for a gun is just another machine.

As to the arming of the workers, the approach of revolutionary struggles has always forced the workers to acquire small arms in their own defence, for the impending struggle has usually been anticipated by Fascist squads, 'Black Hundreds', 'Black and Tans' or other named terrorist bands of the ruling class.

But such arms are few in the aggregate. The chief sources of supply of modern revolutionary forces are the class-conscious units of the army, and the factories. In modern revolutions the munition factories take the place of the armouries and gunsmiths' shops of the 18th and 19th centuries. Not only the munition works, but every engineering factory, workshop or chemical works, is turned to the manufacture or improvisation of weapons.

Highly industrialised countries such as France, Belgium, U.S.A., Germany and others will not suffer the tragic lack of the means of forging arms suffered by agrarian, revolutionary Spain in 1936.

Armchair Socialist theoreticians and Anti-Fascists will sneer at the Workers' Militia and tell us that the barricades of 1848 are outdated, but revolutions have a way of taking these fine weather men unawares. Some years ago the celebrated Anti-Fascist and Liberal Professor Salvemini wrote a learned article against the principle of workers' defence forces. He pointed out that the German Social-Democratic Reichsbanner, the German Communist Rotfront, and similar military organisations of the Liberal and Catholic parties in Germany had surrendered or dissolved without firing a shot when the Nazis took power in 1933. Therefore, reasoned the learned professor, workers' defence corps are useless. The advice of such gentle Anti-Fascists is to call a policeman.

What the professor concealed was that the Social Democratic Reichsbanner and the Communist League of Red Front Fighters did not fight because they were built upon authoritarian principles of orders from above and rigid obedience to leaders. The Socialist leaders were too compromised by political practice to give orders to resist the Nazis. The German Communist leaders were under orders from Moscow, and Stalin wished to, and did, make a treaty with the new Nazi Germany. It was not the principle of workers' defence which failed, but the contrary principle of blind obedience to 'leaders' and the subjection of judgement and self respect to that 'leadership'.

Within a few years of Salvemini's article came the Spanish Fascist uprising of July, 1936. The spontaneous uprising of the workers in defence against Fascism and the rapid organisation of workers' militia, not authoritarian as the German, but federal and Syndicalist, blew to smithereeens the learned discourse of the professor. Life is stronger than theory.

The revolutionary workers everywhere in Spain were rapidly defeating the Fascists when foreign intervention, allowed by the Labour movement of the world, came to the assistance of Franco. The defeat of the Revolution after three years of war was due to that, to the Franco-British policy of 'non-intervention' which allowed arms to Franco, but prevented arms and war supplies reaching the republicans. The efficacy of workers' militia as a defence against Fascist terrorism remains proved by the events of 1936.

We shall anticipate the objections of legalistic Socialists and Liberals who will be ready with tales of 'the streets running with blood and corpses mountain high' by recalling that most revolutions have overthrown the old regime with the loss of a handful of men. The French Revolution of 1789, the overthrow of Tsarism and the October Revolution in 1917, the Austrian and German Revolutions of 1918, were accomplished with an almost unbelievably small roll of casualties.

Of course, if the revolutionaries fight as do the professional armies of states, with a solid front and two armies facing one another with tanks, aircraft and big guns, the revolution would be quickly crushed. But, revolutions cannot be fought like imperialist wars, the social factors are greater than the military. Strategy, tactics and weapons must be designed to wage a social war without fronts.

An excellent case of this is found in the history of the Irish struggle against the British Government during 1919-20 and 1921. The Imperialist forces were increased to about 100,000 men, army, Royal Irish Constabulary, Auxiliaries and 'Black and Tans', with resort to any weapon they needed and the experience of the World War behind them. The Irish Republican Army of about 10,000 armed with automatic pistols, revolvers, home made bombs and a few rifles and machine guns defeated them by adapting their strategy and tactics to the social soil.

Let no one mistake the Workers' Militia for just another army. The Spanish Militia of 1936-37 had no officer caste or badge of rank, no privilege or special ration, no saluting. The ranks were filled, not by conscription, but by the revolutionary knowledge and enthusiasm of the workers. Love of the Revolution took the place of professional military discipline founded on the death penalty. The daily pay was equal to all whether the least experienced militiaman or Durruti.

As well as the Workers' Militia, other bodies of armed men were organised by the Spanish Syndicalists - Frontier Control Committees to prevent the flight of Fascists - and Republican Ministers and Workers' Patrols to prevent disorder or counter-revolutionary outbursts in the towns and villages.

It is obviously necessary for the Revolution to disband the instruments of the old regime, the judges, magistrates and police. But as well as counter-revolutionist attempts, criminal and hooligan elements useless to anyone, may remain as the legacy of capitalism. Indeed the counter-revolutionists will encourage these by bribes, arms and alcohol. The Workers' Patrols organised by the ward and town federations of the Syndicates will easily handle such who would overthrow or discredit the Revolution.

It will be seen that these armed bodies of workers have no resemblance to the forces of the State - capitalist or other. The street patrols will be carried out in the worker's spare time, like firewatching - only of his own free will. The factories and railways will be guarded by armed workers while doing their everyday work. They will continue to carry arms until the need has passed. Then, with no danger present, men will cease to carry arms as they ceased to carry gas masks when they found no danger of gas attack.

But, if, instead of the general force of the workers, the Revolution gives birth to the special force of a new army, police and judiciary, a new state and a new master class will arise. If a new police force were created to arrest counter-revolutionists the policemen would naturally try to preserve their new jobs even when the old regime had been crushed. Let us recall the story of Napoleon's wolves. It is said that while Napoleon was Emperor the number of wolves increased in France, so Napoleon offered a large reward for each wolf's head brought to the local authority. Wolf hunting became a lucrative profession until the wolves began to disappear. Fortunately for the hunters the decline in the wolf population was mysteriously checked and their numbers even began to increase. Upon investigation the authorities discovered that, rather than lose their jobs, the hunters were breeding wolves and even shepherds had turned from their flocks for the more remunerative work of wolf breeding and hunting.

For the defence of the Revolution there must be no new regular army, or police force, or officer caste, but the arming of the workers. If the workers allow themselves to be disarmed, even in the name of the Revolution, then at that moment the counter-revolution has succeeded.

Principles of Syndicalism 9

First Fruits of the Revolution

In this series of articles we have outlined the aim and method of the Syndicalist Revolution. The aim - the abolition of privilege, private property, class society and the State and the establishment of the common ownership of the means of production. The method - the taking and running of industry by workers' Syndicates, the abolition of the standing Army and other armed forces, police, judiciary, etc., and the creation of Workers' Militia and other necessary working class organisation for the administration of society.

But what do we immediately expect from the Revolution? Let us be clear. This is not a plan for a society of a few hundred years hence. We are not making blueprints for our descendants to work to long after we are dead. What we here outline is possible immediately the workers desire it and throw off their chains of illusion. It is the aim of that Revolution which already is stirring in war ridden Europe.

Let us first consider the possibility of man's labour if fruitfully employed. Even in peace time only a small minority of the population is engaged in useful work and even they waste much of their time because of out-of-date machinery and obsolete labour methods. If each did his share of work and took only what he could really enjoy (for who can enjoy a one hundred bedroom mansion or half a dozen motor cars?) it would be necessary to work only a few hours a week for all to enjoy good housing, clothing, food and all the good things of life.

The Revolution would at once set about releasing this unmeasured human labour power. Every fit person would find a socially necessary job. Think of the millions now wasting their time! Capitalists, landowners, parsons, politicians. The domestic, club and restaurant servants of the rich. (Even in wartime one may see two able bodied men opening the double door of a Piccadilly club to allow another able bodied man to pass.) The millions of clerks, bankers and inspectors who count, check and re-check the business of the capitalists. The enormous tax eating Civil Service. The half dozen milkmen in each small street, the vast number of unnecessary shopkeepers and assistants. The collectors and canvassers, the advertising men. All could do useful work and at once make a big stride towards plenty and leisure for all. Here we describe what we consider must be the immediate economic aims of the Revolution.

WAGES. The abolition of wages and the establishment of the principle of equal income for all. What that income would be cannot be expressed in money terms, the only terms known to capitalist society, but it should certainly be more than double the present average wage.

WORK TIME. A six hour working day, a five day week and a month of holidays annually.

OLD AGE, SICKNESS AND BEREAVEMENT. The most generous of proposals and 'demands' for old age pensioners stop well below even the low wages of the workers. Aged workers should receive the same income and services as the younger population. The same is true of the sick and of widows and orphans.

UNEMPLOYMENT. It may be that in the busy, early days of re-organising industry some workers may find themselves temporarily out of work. Unemployment is society's responsibility and the unemployed man should not be punished for it. The equal income of other members of society should be the right of the temporary out-of-work while immediate effort is made to find him a job. We do not believe that any worker will want to shirk his part of the stirring movement of social reconstruction unless he is psychologically or physiologically ill. In any case a job will soon be found and personal adjustment made. It is the capitalist system, alone of social systems, which creates unemployment. Men are unemployed, not because there is no useful work to do, but because a profit cannot at the moment be made from that work. There is always a job to do in a community just as there is always a job to do in the home.

FOOD. The production of a plentiful supply of the best food from our own land. This would need to be of such a character as to radically change the diet of the large majority of the population who eat too much bread and too little eggs, fruit and milk. This production would greatly increase the supply of poultry, eggs, milk, cheese, butter, fruit, fresh salads and vegetables and fish.

We would seek to do this by producing the vastly greater part of our food at home, enjoying it fresh and not robbing the peoples of other lands by the forced imports of finance capital.

To accomplish this we could recruit for the land an extra million workers from the useless jobs they now occupy. We would need to plough up the estates and pleasure grounds of the rich, to reclaim moors and hillsides and other lost land and increase the fertility of most of the present farm land. We would need to fertilise the land by the collection of that valuable 'waste' we now throw away and turn the automobile factories to the production of tractors and other farm machinery. Private land-lordism and rent being abolished no obstacle would stand in the path of this newly released social energy.

MANUFACTURES. The Syndicates would be concerned with the immediate production of sufficient shoes and clothes to meet the reasonable needs of all, with enough house furniture for all and the multiplication of those thousands of goods, wireless sets, books, articles of toilet, sweets, etc., which make life more pleasant. As these flower from the factories in ever-increasing volume the standard of living of all would rise until human saturation point had been reached.

But we are concerned not only with the quantity, but, also, with the quality of goods. Capitalism is the age of shoddy, and shoddy goods are waste. The poor are robbed twice; first from the wage packet, next over the counter by cotton and jute suits, starchy food, gimcrack furniture and leaky shoes. For the first time all workers will enjoy what is now the privilege of the well-to-do, the feel of good cloth, the firm tread of a well-made shoe and the pleasure of well designed goods.

HOUSING. The mainly empty houses of the wealthy must be requisitioned for the housing of the overcrowded. Those houses too big, or otherwise unsuitable for conversion to flats would be used as museums, hospitals, rest-homes and colleges.

It will be urgently necessary to start the immediate building of several millions of houses to meet the shortage and to clear out the slums and semi-slums. This is much easier than might be supposed for there would be no houses of the wealthy or palatial banks, brewers or insurances offices to build and cinemas would take second place. Consider the huge munition factories, the military camps and colossal aerodromes which have been built during the past four years and weigh them against three million houses.

EDUCATION. Education will be free to all able to benefit from it and wishing to enjoy it, free from kindergarten to university. Classes would be smaller, equipment improved and new schools built. The recent trend of education from coercion and terrorism to freedom and co-operation of teacher and scholar would be accelerated.

MEDICINE. Medical treatment would be free - medicine, attendance, clinics and hospitals. But the new society would increase the health of all, not by a new flood of physic, but, in the main, by a better diet, right working and living conditions and the end of industrial fatigue.

RECREATION. The new society would end the petty restrictions which curtail the enjoyment of our few free hours. Moral bigots and publicans close the theatres and cinemas on Sunday, the workers' one free day. Thousands of restrictions prevent him fully enjoying his too short leisure. All these would be swept away. Let each find his pleasure as he will so long as he does not interfere with the freedom and pleasure of others.

66

HOW SOON?

These are the main tasks of our Revolution, tasks which can be accomplished within two or three years of the triumph of the workers' forces. If you, clouded by the pessimism and disappointment of life under capitalism, doubt that statement, then take each item singly and consider, from your own observation and your experience of your job, 'If the waste and profit are cut out, is this thing possible?' We have no doubt of your answer. And this will be but the beginning, but the foundation stone of a free and co-operative society!

Do not ask of us, 'How long will it take to persuade the workers that all this is possible and desirable?' Stop thinking so much of the apathy of the other fellow. When each worker asks the question of himself the Day has dawned.

The Social General Strike

Why 1926 Failed

The repeal of the 1927 Trades Disputes Act by the Labour Parliament makes little difference to the prospect of a General Strike. The Labour leaders believe that, for the present at least, they can better suppress strikes by their control of the trade unions than by Parliament. On the other hand, when the workers are willing to engage the class enemy in a General Strike they will not consult Acts of Parliament to do so. During the 1926 General Strike the strikers did not care two hoots whether the strike was legal or illegal.

Why did the British General Strike of 1926 fail? Not because the workers failed to strike. The number of blacklegs was insignificant. The attempt of the middle-class to scab on the strikers was a poor effort and was rapidly breaking down the machines used. About one per cent of normal train services were running, but only nine days of that caused chaos on the railways for months afterwards. *The breakdown was greater than that caused by the air-raids on London in 1940-41 and took much longer to repair*. The University students and other middle class scabs could not replace the transport workers and certainly did not intend to replace the miners.

Nor did the strike fail because of a fall in the morale of the workers. The aggregate of strikers was much greater on the last day of the strike than on the first and the fighting spirit was much tougher.

The Collapse of Leadership

The strike failed only because it was called off by the trade union leaders and the workers had not learned to distrust those leaders sufficiently. Worse still, the most important divisions of strikers were organised in trade unions and they were used to obeying instructions from the officials of those unions. The strike was betrayed by the leadership.

But do not let us fall into the error of believing that the leaders called off the strike because of their own cowardice. The Labour leaders' economic interests are those of capitalism and in betraying the strike they were defending their economic interest. The trade union leaders never believed in the strike and only led it in order to prevent it being controlled by the workers; they led it in order to ensure its failure. Scores of quotations from the leaders of the Trades Union Congress could be produced

68

to prove this. We have room for but one.

'No General Strike was ever planned or seriously planned as a act of Trade Union policy. I told my own union in April, that such a strike would be a national disaster. . . . We were against the stoppage, not in favour of it.' (*Memoirs*, J. R. Clynes.)

True, the workers were rapidly developing an alternative to the leader principle. The Councils of Action were improvised bodies born of local initiative. Even more significant was the spontaneous and widespread creation of mass picket lines and their unqualified success. But in spite of such a hopeful development the strikers still had the habit of obedience to leaders. It was not, of course, the leaders alone who were defending their capitalist interest inside the Labour movement. The trade unions were not only, through their vast invested funds, shareholders in capitalism - they were part of the social order; as much capitalist institutions as the workhouse or the Houses of Parliament.

To wage a successful General Strike the workers must reject, not only certain leaders, but the leader principle, using to the full their own initiative. They must organise, not in trade unions, but in Syndicalist or revolutionary industrial unions (in Britain the two terms mean the same), and they must change their strategy from that of the General Walk Out Strike to that of the General Stay In Strike.

Stay In Striker

Consider what happens in an orthodox strike, general or particular. The strikers, who had the means of production in their hands one day, on the next hand them over to their class enemies in a nice tidy working condition and go home. The railmen and bus and lorry drivers hand over the vital means of transport, without which modern capitalism and the State cannot exist. The electrical engineers hand over the power stations, the gas workers the gas producers. Dockers, warehousemen and food factory workers surrender millions of tons of precious flour, bacon, meat, butter, rice and fruit. Engineers vacate arsenals which might be used to arm Fascists. Then they go home to sit by grates which gradually become fireless or at tables with a lessening loaf or go out onto the streets to be battened upon their defenceless heads.

How much better to stay at work and do your striking there. Naturally, to many workers this will seem a strange idea, they are used to striking by leaving the job, not by staying on it, least of all to continuing at work and striking at the same time. But stay awhile, all fruitful ideas must have sounded startling at first hearing, as startling as the first steam

69

locomotive to a stage coachman.

Look at it this way. We all depend for our very living upon the machines and those who tend them, the employer even more than we. Not only does he depend upon servants to clean his home and cook his meals, to wash him and dress him and to do everything but chew his food for him, he also depends, far more than we ever shall upon complicated mechanisms, telephones, electric fires, automobiles and so on. There he is vulnerable. Even more vulnerable is his industrial and commercial system and his political institutions.

And behind the machine is a man; he has not yet achieved his dream of Rossum's Universal Robots. That man is the striker - all things are in his hands. Industry is in the workers' hands. They control the trains, the ships and the buses. They run the telephone exchanges and the power stations. They warehouse and prepare the food, clothing, shoes and myriad commodities which make life possible.

In the Social General Strike the workers decide to cut off these supplies from the employing class and to supply them in full - for the first time in history - to the working class.

Instead of starving, we eat as we have never feasted before, instead of being clubbed, shot and imprisoned we retain the means of defending our lives.

The employing class will be without petrol, heat, electricity, communication or servant. Such a General Strike has been often called The General Lockout of the Capitalist Class. Perhaps that is a more appropriate term.

To accomplish such an end, however, the workers must shed the old, outworn methods of trade unionism and adopt those of the Syndicalists and Revolutionary Industrial Unionists. Instead of organising in the branch room of the local Labour Club or the tap room of the 'Red Lion' we must organise on the job; the miners in the pits, the engineers in the factories, the seamen on the ships. Only by organising on the job are we preparing to take over industry. By organising in the trade union local branch we are fitting ourselves for nothing greater than taking over the local dart team.

Let us now consider in greater detail the mode of organisation advocated by Syndicalists for the defence of our class and the taking and holding of industry.

Taking Over

The basis of trade union organisation, as well as its growth and

70

practice, make it unsuited, even dangerous to the taking and running of industry. Trade unions are of three types, trade unions proper, that is craft unions, bastard forms of 'industrial unions' and general mass unions.

Craft unions may have been justified in the days of handicraft production when a craftsman produced, almost entirely alone, the commodity of his trade. Today, however, by the development of technics and the subdivision of labour many crafts and occupations are necessary to the production of even a simple commodity. If we walk into an engineering factory, for instance, we find the workers already organised by the capitalist. The patternmakers work in harmony with the moulders who pass their work to the machinists. The machinists' work is dovetailed into that of the fitters. Maybe blacksmiths, plumbers, coppersmiths, joiners, sheetmetal workers, boilermakers and painters join in the production of this one commodity. Clerks, time-keepers, inspectors and draughtsmen too, are necessary to industrial processes.

Yet while all may be under one roof, producing one type of commodity, say locomotives, these workers may be 'organised' into forty unions. Disorganised would be a more apt word. To ask a Syndicalist: do you believe in trade unionism? is like asking a man if he believes in the penny-farthing bicycle.

However, not all of our engineering workers will be members of craft unions, some will be members of an alleged industrial union, the Amalgamated Engineering Union. The A. E. U. is not a true industrial union for it is organised on the basis of craft not industry, though the craft is given a wider meaning than that of the accepted craft unions. Thus the A. E. U. claims members among marine workers aboard ship, in the chemical industry and scores of other industries and for twenty years has had uneasy relations with the Miners' Federation over its attempts to organise coal-mining workers. In any case, the A. E. U. is not organised on the basis of industry, but upon the basis of residence. That is, if you work in East London and live in West London you will generally be organised, not where you work, but where your bed is.

Redundant Unionism

Besides the craft and pseudo-industrial unions some of the workers will be organised in at least two 'general workers unions', such as the Transport and General or the Municipal and General. These are general unions which 'organise' anybody and everybody, engineers, miners, dockers, busmen, shop assistants, clerks or farm labourers. Anybody and everybody in a vast, amorphous disorderly mass.

71

None of these three types of unionism meets the needs of labour in the modern age. What is needed is a union which will organise the workers of one factory in a single industrial union - craftsmen, labourers, clerks, storekeepers and draughtsmen - male and female - young and old. An industrial union not split into residential areas, but organised on the job, built up inside of the factory.

The organisational plan of revolutionary industrial unionism allows, of course, for complete organisational relations with other factories in the industry. Industrial unions are organised in each industry and service, mining, textiles, rail, education, building, health and so on. All industrial unions are federated into One Big Union. It is intended that the One Big Union shall be a world-wide union of all workers with autonomous administrations in each country.

We have here a plan of union organisation which is capable of running successfully a Social General Strike, of taking and holding industry and locking out the employing class. Not for the General Strike alone must we organise scientifically - the everyday needs of the workers cry aloud for an efficient union movement to protect their wage packets. During these wage struggles and the smaller disputes and tussles which take place daily on the job, the revolutionary unionists are all the time studying their jobs, the technics and organisation of industry. When the occasion to strike occurs they are thus fitted to take and hold the undertaking.

How would the Social General Strike method be applied? On the morning of the strike the revolutionary unionists no longer obey the foremen and managers, each person or gang takes over their own job. Where liaison, delegates or committees are needed such have already been organised.

Who'll Pay the Wages?

Who will pay the wages? No one. Money, the most powerful weapon of the capitalist, is discarded. The banknotes in his wallet are so much fluff. But we must eat to live. Very well, the canning factories, the docks and warehouses are already in the hands of the workers. The flour mills and bake-houses, the dairies and packing houses are controlled by them. The dockers, railwaymen and lorry drivers deliver the food to the factories and working class districts, the shop assistants and canteen workers supply it to the workers and their families.

Distribution will not be according to the amount of money a person has but according to his need. Large families will receive more than small

72

families or single persons. Children will have first call on milk and sweets. Delicacies such as poultry and grapes will go to the hospitals and invalids instead of to wealthy overfed idlers. Farm labourers and small-holders send food to the cities.

Miners will continue to send coal to the surface, and the railwaymens'

industrial union will deliver it to the factories, gasworks, power stations and distribution centres. Power station workers organised in their syndicate will produce electricity and distribute it to the workers' houses, factories and transport undertakings.

Necessary communication among related industrial plants will be the responsibility of the telephone and other Post Office workers.

Distribution

Stores of clothing held by textile mills and shops will be distributed to the most needy by the Textile and Distributive Syndicates. Hospitals and other health service workers will continue their work through their unions. Water and other municipal services will be carried on by the Municipal Workers' Industrial Union.

Newspaper compositors and machinists will refuse any longer to print the lies and provocations of the employing class, as they refused on the eve of the 1926 General Strike in Britain. But instead of walking out of the print shops they remain at work and turn the newspapers into organs of the General Strike.

At a glance any worker can see the obvious advantage of such a strike weapon and its great superiority over the old strike method of starving for three to six months. Superior because we eat instead of starving, but the Syndicalist method is effective not only because of the strikers' seizure of the commissariat for the strikers, it also uses the boycott against the employing class.

All domestic and personal servants who were members of their union would leave their employment. Employers would be forced to cook, make beds, do shopping and run their own errands. Postal workers would cease all communications with bourgeois districts. No buses, trains, trams or lorries would pass through these areas or touch buildings where blacklegs were employed, housed or fed.

No food or drink would be delivered to these places. The municipal workers would strike against sweeping their streets or emptying their dust-bins. Gas, water and electricity would cease to flow to them. The weapons of starvation and deprivation which the capitalists have so often used against the workers would be used against them.

It is obvious that faced with such a situation the employing class will offer anything, a shorter working day, higher wages, holidays with pay, as the French capitalist class did when confronted by the stay-in strikes of the workers of France in 1936. Anything to get back their control of industry.

The greatest mistake the French workers ever made was to hand back to their employers the industries and services they held so successfully. Once having taken control of industry class-conscious industrially organised workers would continue to hold that industry, establishing the principles of common ownership and workers' control of industry, abolishing capitalism and the wages system and distributing the good things of life, each according to his needs.

Stay In Strikes in Europe

The engineering workers of Italy successfully seized the factories in 1920. During the occupation they were fed by the Peasants' Syndicates, co-operatives, distributive workers and railwaymen. After four weeks occupation they returned the factories to the capitalists in return for a shorter working day, a wage increase and several minor concessions; within two years of the return of the factories the workers of Italy were defeated by Fascism.

The workers of France in 1936 took possession of factories and many other undertakings in one of the most successful strikes ever known. Unfortunately they returned them to the employing class in return for holidays with pay, wage increases and a shorter working day. Almost at once the Popular Front government put in power just after the strike by Communist, Socialist and Liberal votes began the piece-meal reconquest of the gains made by the strikers.

Syndicalists have always taught that it is not sufficient to practice the stay-in strike for wage concessions, but that it is necessary to take *and hold* the means of production as the Spanish Syndicalist workers did in 1936. By holding the factories, mines, railways and all means of production and distribution the workers established the principle of Workers' Control of Industry. Each factory is run by the workers of that factory assembled in meeting and by the delegates elected by them, such delegates to be subject to instant recall by the people who elected them should they not fulfil their duties. Each factory or group of workshops is, in the same way, represented on the district council of its industry. Each district is represented on the national council

74

of the industry. All industries and services are federated to a National Council of Labour integrating the whole social economy of the country, distributing work and materials, cutting out waste, preparing statistics and assessing distribution.

By this means the social economy is integrated without centralisation, that clumsy red-tape bound machine of the bureaucrat. By having the affairs of an industry controlled by the persons working in that industry, by district affairs being controlled by the district and factory affairs by the workers in that factory; by control from below instead of from above and by exercising the principle of election and recall, federalism, instead of centralism, becomes the principle of the new society.

Do We Need Foremen?

Some say to us: 'But, you will still need foremen.' We do not agree. A workman who knows his job does not need a foreman - a workman who does not know his job needs the advice and help of his mates. In any case a foreman is rarely appointed because of his superior knowledge or gift of leadership. Marriage, membership of certain clubs, drinking, fawning and bluff, all may open the door to promotion. However, if 'foremen' were necessary under Workers' Control, we do not pretend to be able to forecast every detail of the new society, but this we do know, any 'foreman' or such person would be appointed by the men and be subject to their recall.

Here we see a new principle at work - control from below. At present, and in a State Socialist society, all promotion is from above downwards. We see what the latter means at our work. If a foreman of mediocre ability is about to promote some one from the bench to the chargehand's desk and he spots a worker of outstanding ability who would make a much better foreman than he, does he promote that worker? Hardly! To do so would be to prepare his own downfall, certainly to endanger his own job, so he usually promotes somebody who will not be a serious rival. So it goes on, right up to the top - selection by mediocrity! The worker is usually able to recognise a fellow worker's outstanding skill and acknowledge it. The workers would have no social or economic motive in keeping a good man down, instead, it would be in their interest to nominate him to more responsible work.

Having said that, under the principle of social ownership, the miners would control the mines and engineers the metal working factories, we are often asked: But who would run the hospitals and who would look

75

after municipal services such as water supply? Of course hospitals would be run by the hospital workers, all of them, organised in the Health Workers' Syndicate. Municipal services, such as water supply and street cleansing, would be the responsibility of the Municipal Workers' Syndicate. Similarly, education would be the responsibility of those who had spent their lives studying and practicing the art of pedagogy. Of course, the workers of these three syndicates would work in co-operation with the patients, house-dwellers, scholars and parents respectively.

Here is a system of industrial democracy, the only true democracy, not the choice of choosing Tweedledum or Tweedledee every five, eight or ten years and being controlled by him and his partners for the period between, but the control of one's own job and environment, the control of one's own life. The government of men by men gives way to the administration of things.

As to distribution, the Syndicalist method of distribution is free; a system of common ownership and Workers' Control must have a system of free and common distribution to supplement it. That is, all the good things of life will be produced in plentiful supply and distributed by the distributive, municipal and transport workers to whomever needs them, as much as he needs them. Just as now a person may borrow from the public library as many books as he needs, so he will be allowed as much food as he can eat without payment. Once one had to pay to cross bridges, enter parks and even walk along roads, now we may do that freely. So in a Syndicalist society cinemas and theatres will be as free as museums or parks; railways, trams and postage will be as free of charge as roads and bridges are now.

Some will say that the greedy will eat too much if there is enough for all. Well, water is probably the most precious of commodities, in use value that is, but any one will give a thirsty stranger a glass of water - a pailful if he can drink it. No one worries about some one drinking more than his share of water. Certainly no one hoards pails of water in miserly style, for water being freely to hand, appeals not to the miser or glutton. If bread were as plentiful as water, who would eat more than his share?

Power to the Workers

'But you would still have criminals and hooligans.' Yes, we would still be pestered for a few years by these dregs of capitalist society, and the workers would know how to protect their new won society from these miserable misfits and from counter-revolutionists and Fascists. The workers' Syndicates would establish Workers' Militias as did the Spanish workers in 1936, workers' patrols and whatever other means of workers' defence were necessary. If needful, the Syndicates would arm their militias. But that would not be state power-politics, for the state is the special force of public repression used by the ruling class, old or new, against its subjects the people. The armed Syndicates would be a general force - a people in arms. After a while it would be unnecessary for workers to carry arms and these would gradually be laid away, as people during the late war laid aside their gas masks when they discovered that no gas attack was likely. Full freedom would be born and develop naturally and in its own time.

How different when the Revolution gives birth to a new state as in France in 1789 and Russia in 1917. In Russia, for example, power came into the hands of the Bolshevik Party, who used it to disarm the workers and build a regular army, police force, secret political police and use spies, gaolers and judges to maintain their political power. In a political revolution power is in the hands of a ruling party. In a social revolution power is in the hands of the workers. If the workers allow themselves to be disarmed by a new government then counter-revolution succeeds.

The Syndicalist Social General Strike then aims at the conquest of the means of production by the workers. We are now poor and enslaved not because of lack of reforms made by politicians, but because the employing class own and control the means of production, without access to which we cannot live. So long as others control the means whereby we live so long shall we be slaves. Only by taking and holding the means of production can the workers be free.

What's Wrong with the Unions?

There are several ways of beginning a book or pamphlet on a labour question. One may start, as many pundits do, with Adam and Eve and work on through history until one has reached the Tolpuddle martyrs on the second last page. Or one might begin, continue and end by quoting the writings of bearded gentlemen who lived a hundred years ago. This method saves writing half of the book if sufficient quotations are made - and it saves all the ideas. The pen may be mightier than the sword, but the scissors beats both of them!

There is a third method. . . .to begin with the subject at its place and in its time. This I would do. I will take as my starting point a discussion I had with my workmates a few days ago. This discussion is woven, in my remembrance, into many other discussions, for they have had the same theme and have ended without solution. And the subject has probably often been discussed by you and your mates, be you miner, clerk, bus driver or machinist. 'What's wrong with the unions?'

Midwives and Gravediggers

Perhaps the most talked about union at the moment is the Transport & General Workers' Union - that big, ungainly and redoubtable animal. All seem to agree that it's far too big and too undemocratic. Some would destroy it at once, others would reform it, and a few rejoice at its dismemberment into more homely portions.

But many older members of the union, remembering past labour struggles, hesitate to attack its fabric. The oldest dockers, for example, remember the days when their calling was the most depressed of any, when wages were very low, work casual and always uncertain; when men were often, in their hunger, forced to fight like animals for a day's work, and when the pub-owning stevedore robbed them of half their miserable wage.

They contrast those days with their later position, especially after 1920, when wages rose above those of many skilled men, the 'slave' market was curtailed and most of the old abuses abolished. These men say: 'Without our union this could not be. As clumsy as it is, we don't want to wreck it.' Certainly, without the struggle, the solidarity and the discipline of the dockers' organisation, these fruits would not have been gathered.

A similar, though less dramatic story, is told of the London busmen,

78

the unskilled factory labourers, women industrial workers and others. Organisation and strike action have raised their living standard and their position in society.

But these replies, sincere as they are, do not meet the main objection. The T. & G. W. U. is a huge union, formed by amalgamation and a policy of recruiting 'everybody from midwives to gravediggers,' and the brightest battle honours on the union's flag belong to pre-amalgamation days. The dockers' greatest victories, for example, were achieved by the old Dockers' Union, before it was swallowed by the T. & G. W. U.

Now this union is a colossus which strides the country. It is big, unwieldy, unresponsive to the changing needs of its members, undemocratic, with appointed organisers and irritatingly clumsy and slow.

The Outcasts Rise!

But these faults are not held alone by the Transport Union. Other unions are similarly clumsy and huge, and the reason for these things may be found in the earlier development of labour unionism in Britain. The present trade union movement (I leave out the earlier, abortive attempts to form unions) was in its initial stages limited to the miners and the skilled craftsmen. The others were ignored for years. So trade unionism became, except for the miners, craft unionism.

Then came the organisation of dockers, tramwaymen, lorry drivers and general labourers. Organised at first in particular unions, such as the dockers, and in amorphous collections of unskilled labourers, they tended to amalgamate without any defined boundaries, such as are natural to a mining community or a strictly sectarian craft.

In some cases the new labourers' unions organised definite groups of workers, such as the tramwaymen and dockers, but soon most of their membership was spread throughout all industries - engineering, farming, milk distribution and a hundred others. Because the craft unions in these industries refused to organise unskilled labour, there was no choice for the lowest paid workers but to join a general labourers' union.

Having demonstrated that 'unity is strength,' it seemed right and proper to these new unionists to amalgamate the several general unions into larger and ever more general organisations, until two unions, the Transport & General Workers' Union and the National Union of General and Municipal Workers numbered most of the unskilled, and even some skilled unionists on their books. The result was the overgrown, unwieldy, undemocratic and shapeless crowds which these unions now are.

But these unions did, nevertheless, raise the wages and the social

79

standing of their members, especially in relation to the skilled craftsmen. For example, in 1914 a skilled worker in engineering or shipbuilding in such towns as Glasgow or Newcastle received 37 shillings without providing his own tools; his mate or labourer received 18 shillings. In 1924 the skilled rate in such towns for these industries was 1 shilling 2 1/2 pence an hour, but unskilled dockers received 1 shilling and sixpence an hour. Of course, there was a social tendency in that direction, but union organisation was needed to exploit and complete that tendency.

Having completed its historic task of raising the unskilled worker, the general union has now reached a dead end. With its present basis, no further development seems possible. Its members are either apathetic or discontented, and breakaways are ever more frequently threatened.

The Craft Unions

The position of the craft union is scarcely better. It seeks to justify itself by organising men on a social basis which is mediaeval rather than twentieth century. Its basis is not the factory or industry a man works in, or the commodity he helps to produce, but the tools he uses - and even, in some cases, the tools he once used. This had some meaning a few hundred years ago, for men in one small workshop, using a kit of tools, might produce one complete commodity, as did the coachbuilders, coopers or shipwrights.

It was natural, then, to organise men according to the tools they used. . . .capenters, blacksmiths, shoemakers, tailors, cutters, goldsmiths. But now many tools and crafts are needed to produce even one commodity. For one engineering product, the work of moulders, fitters, machinists, electricians and a score of others comes into play. And not only tradesmen, but semi-skilled and unskilled labour (if we may use these rapidly fading definitions) and office labour too (draughtsmen and book-keepers).

Yet the old union demarcations persist - like the Lord Mayor's Show a relic of another age. In an engineering shop where a few hundred or few thousand workers produce but one commodity, 40 or 50 unions may claim to organise the workers. Not only the craft unions, but the general unions, lapping like the sea over broken dykes, claiming a large slice of union membership behind their banners: 'We organise everybody from midwives to gravediggers.' Yet all claim that this mess is organisation and shout: 'Unity is strength.'

The simple truth is that the craft union was formed to fight a war on two fronts - against the employer and against other workers. It bargained with the employer to get the highest price for its labour. To increase its bargaining power, it sought to curtail the supply of the commodity it was selling by restrictions, such as a long and low-paid apprenticeship. It kept out the worker who had not served his time and fought other crafts to maintain its monopoly of certain processes and even sought to nibble at the preserves of other unions. Thus, in a situation which demanded the highest degree of class solidarity and consciousness, the skilled unions have been little more than limited liability companies selling labour power.

More conservative than the Tories, the craft unions tried to hold on to their exclusive and sectarian positions in a changing economy which fast made them obsolete. Machinery has broken down many craft barriers, two world wars have opened the gate to a flood of unapprenticed labour, and social and political development has swept away social differences of skilled and unskilled. Yet most craft unions go on clinging to a fast diminishing tradition. Like the Bourbons, they forget nothing and learn nothing.

Sect or Industry?

What is the alternative to craft unionism and crowd unionism? Let us take a walk through a factory - say an engineering shop producing locomotives. We start in the drawing office, go on through the pattern shop, then the foundry, on to the machine shop, visit stores and minor workshops, finally passing through the fitting and erecting shops. How true must seem our earlier statement that all of these, say, 2,000 workers are united in producing one single commodity. Each is necessary to the other; a single process operates from gate to gate.

Yet in this one factory, in the jackets hanging behind bench and machine, are the membership cards of 20 to 40 different unions- all probably bearing such inscriptions as: 'United we stand, divided we fall,' or 'Unity is strength!' Some may even carry a picture of a small boy watching his grandfather vainly trying to break a bundle of firewood, and its companion picture showing the old man, who has now tumbled to the trick, breaking them one by one, much to the child's relief.

Unfortunate men! They are united in their work and divided in their unions.

Now it must seem obvious that all men and women in this one factory should belong to one union, whatever their craft, whether they be skilled or unskilled, male or female. The clerical and drawing office staff, too, should be organised in this one engineering workers' union.

The industry, the commodity produced, gives a good, easy basis of union organisation. A worker going from one engineering factory to another finds himself on familiar ground within a few hours and usually understands the problems of other workers like himself fairly easily. The limits of the industry, then, should generally be the limits of the unions. It would obviously be foolish to suggest that the engineering union should organise farm labourers or miners or midwives into its ranks. Yet some unions spread themselves over even more diverse occupations than these.

False Industrial Unions

The syndicalist propaganda for industrial unionism has, in some industries, been met by the transformation of some craft unions into false industrial unions. Most prominent of these is the Amalgamated Engineering Union, which opened its doors first to the semi-skilled, then the unskilled and, a few years ago, the women workers,

But the A. E. U. is not an industrial union. It has not succeeded in amalgamating the many craft unions in the engineering trade, yet it seeks to organise sections of workers in almost every industry - building, electricity, milk processing, chemicals and many others, even where a union claiming to be industrial is organising most of the workers. For some years the A. E. U. has been in dispute with the miners' union, because the latter claims all workers in the mining industry.

There are other unions, such as the Electrical Trades Union, which have a similar double basis - to seek to organise a large slice of one industry and fragments of all the rest.

The Syndicalist conception of industrial unionism is certainly not that of the A. E. U., E. T. U. or other so-called industrial unions. We believe in one union only for one industry. But revolutionary industrial unionism means more than that - it has its beginning, its foundation, in industry. Most unions - the miners' is an exception - are organised on a doss-house basis. A doss-house is not concerned about where a man works, but only where he sleeps, and most trade unions organise their members according to their place of residence. If a London A. E. U. member works in a factory in Acton, but lives in Willesden, he will usually join a Willesden branch of the A. E. U. His fellow workers in the Acton shop will, similarly, be organised by branches in the localities where they sleep - perhaps a hundred branches in 30 or 40 places, often 20 miles apart.

One result of this seemingly convenient arrangement is the unsuitability of the branch meeting as a means of discussing workshop problems, for our member may, when he goes to his branch at Willesden or Poplar, be in the company of men who work in scores of different factories or even industries, and are unwilling to devote the whole of an evening to discussing his particular place of work. One may see the result of this in the dull, lifeless business routine of trade union branch meetings and in the irrelevant matters they discuss.

The place to start the industrial union branch is industry - the factory, mill, mine, shop or office. Every worker in the factory should be a member of the one branch, or sub branch where the factory is very large. The branch should meet at, or near, the factory, and the secretary, treasurer and shop stewards be elected from the factory. In such a branch, all matters relating to the particular factory could be discussed in an atmosphere of understanding and interest.

District Federation

But a worker's problems are not limited to the place where he works, I can hear someone say. That is true, and the factory branch is only the beginning of Syndicalism. In all things which are particular to our factory, the branch has autonomy, but there are other problems which may concern, say, similar factories in the same district. This presents no difficulty, however, for the industrial branch will be federated to the district federation of engineers - or miners - or railwaymen.

It is surprising how, on reflection, we find certain industries fall into fairly distinct districts. . . .Lancashire cotton, West Riding wool, London transport, Durham coal and so on. Here the superiority of Syndicalist over territorial organisation will be seen, for a district of one industry in, say, the West of Scotland, will overlap and underlap that of other industries. The organisational basis of Syndicalism is adaptable to this, but the territorial method, such as that of parliamentary groupings, has to squeeze, lop off and fill up to make its rigid pattern on the political map.

Look at any population map. You will see how, while people live together in moderately defined regions, their work districts overlap each other.

Now, while the district federation of the industry deals with things which are peculiar to the industry of its district, and not the special concern of one particular factory, there are problems which can be solved only on a national or country-wide basis. Just as the branch has autonomy over its own affairs, but federates to the district to tackle more general questions, so the district federation of each industry is federated to its national federation of engineers - or textile workers - or chemical workers.

83

Up to now we have 30 or so industrial unions or federations and I can hear some of our critics crying that we have left labour still divided, but again the Syndicalist principle of federation goes to work. The industrial federations deal with those questions that are peculiar to each of their industries, but some problems may concern more than one industry - such as a strike of railwaymen directly concerning busmen, and there are questions which affect all workers, whatever their industry. So there comes about the federation of all industrial unions on a national scale - the National Federation of Labour.

National Federation of Labour

The National Federation is a gathering of all the strength and counsel of the industrial federations, covering every industry and service - mines, factories, power stations, offices, schools, hospitals, railways, shipping. . . . It is able to swing its forces from one front to another, to aid any one section of labour by the solidarity of whatever other sections are needed.

Such a federation is quite different to the present Trades Union Congress, which has rarely been more than an annual consultative meeting and has long since degenerated into a political debating society.

As well as federation on a national scale, some form of general local organisation is necessary. Quite simply, the industrial branches of each union join together in a local federation in each city, town or farming district. While this may seem somewhat akin to the existing trades councils, there is an important distinction. Trades councils are, in the main, rather loose federations of trade union branches formed on a residential basis and, in any case, are usually confused as to their exact function, become bogged down in local politics and can rarely distinguish themselves from the local Labour Party and its functions.

The Syndicalist local federation, on the other hand, is largely a body of delegates from factories and other places of work in or about the town and is concerned with truly labour problems, rather than who shall wear the mayor's brass chain next year or who shall be nominated as the town's dog-catcher.

Delegates

While Syndicalists look to the elemental mass meeting of the workers at their place of work as the foundation of organisation and the

84

greatest source of labour's strength, there are, nevertheless, certain functions which cannot be carried out by a mass meeting - certain details and arrangements where delegation of function is necessary. So the meeting elects delegates to carry out its wishes and general resolutions.

But these men and women are nothing *but* delegates. They are elected for certain limited functions, to carry out certain general instructions, and always subject to recall. The right of recall is fundamental to Syndicalism, though it is somewhat strange to the orthodox labour movement and completely foreign to the Communist belief.

It is the simple principle that whoever elects may recall, whoever gives may take away. A delegate is elected to carry out a certain function or policy; if he disregards the wishes of his fellow workers, then they may at once recall him. How the trade-union movement has suffered from neglect of this principle, which trade-union leaders and would-be bosses have always disliked.

The nearest the trade unions have come to it is in the shop steward movement, but for years the Communists - often with considerable success - have fought fiercely against this principle, seeking to make each Communist shop steward a *papier-mache* Stalin and even denying the workers the right to make strike decisions.

But the Syndicalist stands firmly by these things - the mass meetings, delegates not bosses, the right of recall. Here, indeed, is the hallmark of Syndicalism.

It is now evident that Syndicalism is organised from the bottom upwards - the factory, the mass meeting, the delegate - and that all power comes from below and is controlled from below. This is a revolutionary principle, one of the few truly revolutionary principles advocated in the twentieth century. In all other movements, government, regulation, is from above downwards. The capitalist, the dictator, the leader, the hereditary boss tells his flock what they must do - strictly in their own interests, of course! But he decides what is good and what is evil. All movements so based, even if claiming to be revolutionary, are founded upon the concept of slave and master - though maybe a self-styled kind master. Only Syndicalism is based on free men.

All parties, capitalist or 'labour', and all social relationships except Syndicalism, are at one in opposing the principle of control from below. All are willing to fight to the last ditch to preserve the principle of control from above, the relation of master and servant. Communism, Conservatism, Labourism, capitalism, business (big or small) - all are bound and rooted in the master principle, as were the previous systems of feudalism and chattel slavery.

The Syndicalist principle of control from below, then, is truly revolutionary and, as such, is repulsive to the political parties and excites the anger of groups and individuals who wish to appear revolutionary while, at the same time, they retain the principles of a conservative society.

Control from below runs through all Syndicalist manifestations - its organisation, its activity and its idea of a future society.

The Right To Strike

In our strike activity, we find ourselves at once in conflict with the Communist Party, which denies the right of the worker to make his own decisions. To us, the decision to strike or not to strike belongs, as a group agreement, to the workers concerned in a dispute. It is for them, as a collective body, to decide when to strike and when to return.

To this principle, the Communist official will bow only when he is forced, or - as most often happens - when, having made a fiasco of a strike he has called, he is anxious to get the strikers back to work before his ill-judged and mismanaged skirmish collapses. Then he will call on the workers to vote, 'to make their own decision', knowing full well that only one decision is possible in the circumstances he has created.

In unions over which the Communists have gained control, the officials have taken from the members the right to strike and vested it in themselves, so that the workers are like cannon-fodder at the disposal of generals.

A worker who has not the right to strike is less than a man, he is a slave. Only this right raises him above the beasts of burden.

Knowing this, Syndicalists have always fought in its defence. In the unions, in capitalist society, in Franco Spain as in Fascist Italy and Bolshevik Russia, they have defended the right to strike.

The strike, the withdrawal of labour power in varied ways, is not the only weapon of working-class struggle, but it is the chief one - and the basis of others. By striking, however, we do not necessarily mean the conventional method of long negotiation, several months notice and then a withdrawal of labour into the streets, to await the result of a long, drawn-out struggle in ever-increasing poverty.

Certainly, such a struggle may have to be faced, but other methods, quicker and not so painful, are quite often open to the workers. Such ways have been thought out, used and developed by Syndicalists of many countries, with great success. The lightning strike, 'work to rule,' the 'strike at work,' the boycott, the sympathetic strike, the guerilla and the stay-in strike are Syndicalist weapons, which even trade unionists have learned to use with excellent results, Syndicalist propaganda having made them familiar to thousands.

Let us consider, briefly, the nature of some of the Syndicalist strike tactics. The lightning strike, not alone because of its speed, but also as a result of the time and place of its blow, is usually more effective than the orthodox, long drawn-out affair, played according to a set of rules almost as traditional as those of chess. It is particularly effective on a small scale, as in a single factory or group of factories. Here again, the rght of the workers to decide is important for the worker on the spot usually knows better than any remote official when is the right time, where is the right place to use the lightning strike. Only he knows all the many, often minute conditions which will determine its success or failure.

The practice of guerilla strikes has been tried in England by one orthodox trade union, with some success, but this experiment was but a pale imitation of the red-blooded Syndicalist method. The guerilla strike is particularly well suited to certain industries, such as engineering, which are of a diverse character. Even in the pre-war days of slump, some sections of engineering, were quite prosperous - aircraft, for instance - while other sections, such as shipbuilding, were in the lowest depths of industrial misery.

Yet wages for the whole industry were based on its most depressed section. Obviously, here was a case for obtaining better conditions as time, place and circumstance allowed, winning a pound in this town or ten shillings in that factory. Certainly this was tried, with some success, but in every case the workers concerned found themselves in conflict with their unions, who had all made agreements fixing national wage scales and outlawing guerilla strikes.

One of the foundation principles of Syndicalism is the sympathetic strike, but for a hundred years this principle has had but a flickering life in Britain. How many times have we seen strikers defeated, not by the employers, but by their organised trade-union brethren, who blacklegged against them? Busmen against railmen; London tube men against London busmen working for the same company; ship repair workers on strike and members of the dockers' union and the National Union of Seamen taking the ships to be repaired in France or Holland; iron moulders on strike, while machinists and fitters worked scab castings.

So the unhappy tale might go on. Only recently have we seen the faint beginning of the sympathetic strike in England. A lot more Syndicalist propaganda is needed to bring it to fruit, and a Syndicalist form of federal organisation is needed to make it work effectively. Then shall we realise the strength of the historic slogan of the I. W. W. (Industrial Workers of the World): 'An injury to one is the concern of all.'

The Boycott

Akin to the sympathetic strike is the boycott, little used by union - apart from the strong Syndicalist organisations of Spain and Sweden. It is worthwhile recalling the origins of the term boycott.

In the fight of the Irish peasants against the landlords, the tenant farmers formed the Irish Land League. The landlords were evicting tenants who could not pay their increased rents, and replacing them with new tenants. The League forbade farmers to occupy the farms of evicted peasants, but some farmers defied this order.

Then the League used its greatest weapon, against which the landlords, the magistrates and the military were helpless - the boycott. Farm labourers and house servants left these farms, the cows went un-milked and crops rotted in the fields. The carter, the grocer, the butcher, even the doctor and the undertaker refused their services to the boycotted farmers.

Successful as it was in early nineteenth century Ireland, how much more victorious can this weapon be in our modern, complex society. The boycott can be used by certain sections of industrial workers, in particular transport men, to support other striking groups, but it can also be used in a general-public way to aid strikers in public service by blacklisting the disputed concern's goods and services. Newspapers, shops, cinemas, theatres, laundries, coal merchants and life insurance are examples which spring quickly to mind.

Many ingenious strike tactics have been invented by the French Syndicalists. Of these, the work-to-rule strike of the railmen is, perhaps, best known. When, under nationalisation, French railway strikes were forbidden, their Syndicalist felows were delighted to urge the railmen to carry out the strict letter of the law. Now French railways, like those of most other countries, are governed by thousands of laws, most of them unused and ignored, their place being taken by commonsense and experience.

But the French railmen worked to the rule-book. The railway laws were carried out just as the government said they ought to be.

One French law tells the engine-driver to make sure of the safety of any bridge over which his train must pass. If, after personal examination, he is still doubtful, then he must consult the other members of the train's crew. Of course, trains ran late!

Another law for which French railmen developed a sudden passion related to the ticket collectors. All tickets had to be examined thoroughly on both sides. The law said nothing of city rush hours. The results of working to rule were to tie up the railways, make the law look an ass and win the railmen's cause.

It is interesting here to recall that groups of English Syndicalist workers on the old North Eastern Railway carried out this tactic about 35 years ago with complete success.

More recently, largely as a result of Syndicalist propaganda, London busmen have, with great success, tried this method.

Good Work Strike

A similar Syndicalist strike tactic is the good work strike. Workers, particularly in Spain, who were building cheap working-class houses, put best workmanship into even shoddy materials. Doors hung straight, windows opened and shut, roofs were waterproof and walls perpendicular.

The most amusing case of this form of strike action comes from the U. S. A. and concerns an accusation made against the militant union, the I. W. W. In a canning factory, the labels for the tins are said to have been mixed, so that poor people buying what they thought was cheap pink salmon, were delighted to get sock-eye steaks. From the poor districts came orders for more of that salmon, while from better-off districts came bitter rebukes and insults.

Many other examples of Syndicalist strike strategy might be given, had we the space, but enough has been said to show that Syndicalists are not committed to only one strike method, but adapt their tactics to the time and place, so that the greatest victory may be won by the least amount of human suffering.

But all such ways of striking are skirmishes before the real battle, training for the most powerful of Syndicalist weapons - the stay-in strike.

Stay-in Strike

The workers, instead of walking out and leaving the factory or other plant in the hands of the employer, stay in and lock out the boss. This at once prevents the factory being used for blacklegging and protects the strikers.

This method was tried by the automobile workers of Detroit and other parts of the United States in 1937. There, stikers had suffered defeat by using the conventional strike method, principally because their picket lines had been battered by the police and by employers' gangs. But in 1937, by 'seizing' the car factories, they at once made the strike blackleg-proof. They were no longer assaulted by the police, for now they were barricaded in the factories. The strike was completely successful in a few weeks.

But Spain, France and Italy, with their strong Syndicalist traditions, give us the best-known examples of the widespread stay-in strike. In France, the last occasion of its use on a nation-wide scale was June, 1936. To combat falling wages, the engineering workers declared a strike and seized the factories. They were quickly followed by millions of others, even by saleswomen in the fashionable shops.

The stay-in strike action - swift, widespread and determined - at once arrested the downward trend of wages and gained solid increases on previous rates. It also gained for most workers the forty-hour week, holidays with pay and other improvements. Shortly after this sweeping victory by workers' direct action, there came into being the notorious 'People's Front' Government of Liberals, Communists and Socialists. Abroad, this government was given the credit for the workers' gains of 1936 by lying Popular Front propaganda, although the 'People's' Government was elected *after* the event.

This government, as must be expected of any such reactionary combination, at once began to gnaw away at the workers' gains by acts of legislation, until most of them had been lost and the way prepared, first for industrial conscription, then for the Vichy government. Remember, the Vichy fascist government of 1940 was built on the foundations laid by the reactionary 'People's' Government, after the French workers had relinquished the proven weapon of direct action for the paper sword of political action.

An Italian Lesson

Italy in 1920 gives us another example of large-scale stay-in strike action. This, too, began in the engineering factories. The Italian engineering employers had demanded a substantial reduction of wages and, meeting refusal, decided on a lock-out. The engineering workers, with a strong Syndicalist minority, decided to use the chief Syndicalist weapon. Telephone and telegraph wires hummed, couriers and motor-cyclists sped through the night and, in one swift, co-ordinated action, the metal factories were seized by the workers.

Other industries at once responded. Railwaymen and road transport men moved supplies. Food was provided by the workers in bakeries and flour mills, by the co-operatives and by the peasant organisations. Post Office and telephone workers maintained communications among the many factories 'on strike'.

But what of the government, the army and the police? Railwaymen were willing to refuse to move any soldiers under arms or any military supplies. The police were helpless, for the strikers were barricaded in the factories, surrounded by barbed wire and electrified steel fences.

At that time in Italy there was a strong, well-armed Fascist miltary organisation, but it was helpless against the stay-in strike. The workers had the means to arm themselves in defence against the blackshirts - steel, forges and machines. Mussolini looked on, powerless to intervene.

George Seldes, in his best-selling biography of Mussolini, *Sawdust Caesar*, writes of this strike:-

'Not a skull was cracked. Not a safe. . . .Commotion everywhere, except in Italy. It is true that, day by day, more and more factories were being occupied by the workers. Soon 500,000 'strikers' were at work, building automobiles, steamships, forging tools, manufacturing a thousand useful things, but there was not a shop or factory owner there to boss them or to dictate letters in the vacant offices. Peace reigned.'

The Italian workers were victorious. The employers withdrew their demands for wage cuts and, instead, offered increases and other concessions. Unfortunately, the workers accepted these offers and, against the advice of the Syndicalist minority, handed back the factories. They enjoyed their gains for a little while, then reaction began nibbling at the gains of 1920, until, two years later, the workers - weak without their factory fortresses and their direct action spirit, and debilitated by political propaganda - were defeated.

Again the political fabulists click their typewriters, falsifying history, and political speakers, by malice and by ignorance, propagate falsehood, declaring that the Blackshirts expelled the strikers from the factories and instituted the Fascist State from that action.

In truth, Mussolini, who at the beginning of the strike loudly opposed it, soon fell silent and took no action against it, mute and awed as he was by the mighty force of workers, conscious for a brief hour of their great strength. The stay-in strike was in 1920; the Fascists gained power in 1922, after the Italian workers had relied on political action for their defence. Two years of history are thus neatly clipped out by the scissors of 'progressive' political propagandists, in their attempts to discredit the stay-in strike.

Of course the workers were wrong in the limited use they made of this strike weapon. They ought to have retained the factories and extended the strike to all industries, using it as the basis of a new society.

Blind-alley Unionism

The greatest weakness of the trade union movement is its lack of an ultimate aim. Created to secure a higher wage and a shorter working day, it achieved its aims and now finds itself at the blind end of a limited path. Its own members are becoming dissatisfied with such a circumscribed social function. In any case, the usefulness of wage advances in conditions of inflation is increasingly questioned, yet, at the same time, the permanence of the capitalist system is accepted.

Wage increases and rising prices make the trade union movement look like a dog chasing its own tail. The constant scrabble for paper pennies has even led to the abandonment of the shorter working week and the eight-hour ideal of 70 years ago. True, on paper we have a 44 hour week - on paper - but systematic overtime is becoming almost universal and is even established in some trade union agreements. It is often said that some people were in favour of the 44 hour week only because their overtime would start sooner.

Here is the end of trade union thought. It can no more think itself into a further stage of social development than a man can lift himself by his own shoestrings.

The trade union is designed to function only in a commodity society, where everyone is selling something, and in which the worker has only his labour power to sell. The price of commodities rises and falls with changes in supply and demand and the price of the commodity, labour power - wages - also rises with an increase in the demand for labour, as we see at the present time. But, with an increase of the labour supply beyond the needs of the market, wages fall. British labour's wages, however, are not governed alone by national conditions, but, more than most countries, by international factors. Changes in India, Japan, the U. S. and Australia are, almost at once, felt in Britain.

It is in this world market society that trade unions function and beyond which they have no hope or knowledge. It is true that many unions have in their rule-books a preamble in favour of the nationalisation, or even socialisation, of the means of production and distribution, but such declarations have no more significance than the dubious Latin inscriptions on coats of arms.

The trade union is not designed or organised for any higher function than selling labour power in a labour market.

A New Society

Any major advance by labour can be achieved only by escaping from the bonds of the wages system, and that means a radical change in the social order - a change from private to social ownership and the designing of production for men's needs, instead of for their fluctuating purchasing power.

But it is just here, in the contemplation of an alternative to capitalism, that the trade union stops dead. Negotiate an extra threepence an hour or question the redundancy of some machinists, yes.... but a new society? That is like asking a fish to move on dry land.

A society such as we desire, based on the economic and emotional needs of all, and not of a ruling class, must have an economic and not a political foundation. As Jim Connolly so often quoted:

'There is not a socialist in the world to-day who can indicate with any degree of clearness how we can bring about the co-operative commonwealth except along the lines suggested by industrial organisation of the workers.

'Political institutions are not adapted to the administration of the co-operative commonwealth that we are working for. Only the industrial form of organisation offers us even a theoretical constructive socialist programme. There is no constructive socialism except on the industrial field.'

Syndicalism, distinct from orthodox trades unionism, regards wage struggles not as principle ends, but as secondary aims and means to a greater end - the abolition of the wages system and the creation of a new society. The organisation of Syndicalism, in industrial unions, is in harmony with this end. The strike strategy of Syndicalism, leading to the social stay-in strike, is true to the ideal of a society of free men.

While its aim in every wage struggle is to win that limited fight, at the same time it uses the struggle to enlighten and raise the confidence and fighting ability of the workers for the greatest struggle of all, when we shall demand, not the half-loaf which is said to be better than no bread, but the whole bakehouse.

So long as labour is a commodity - something for sale on a labour market - subject to a variable economic climate, the worker will remain a slave. Not a slave serving one particular master, but the slave of a master class. At the best of times his living will be determined by his commodity basis and limited by the 'cost of living.' At the worst, it will sink, in times of economic depression, to starvation and misery, even in a world of plenty. Atomic power and space travel will still find him trudging the streets seeking work, or sitting by a fireless grate. The worker can become master of his fate only when he has become master of the machine.

But it is obvious that private ownership of the means of production cannot be spread over millions of persons. Private ownership of factories, mines and modern transport systems is possible only for the few. When the many control the means whereby they live, they will do so by abolishing private ownership and establishing common ownership of the means of production, with workers' control of industry.

This is not to be confused with nationalisation and state control, which has been well described as 'the government of the people, by the Civil Service, for the Civil Service.'

Where ownership is, in theory, said to be vested in the people, but control is in the hands of a small class of bureaucrats, then common ownership does not exist, but the labour market and wage labour go on, the worker remaining a wage slave to State capitalism.

Common ownership demands common control. This is possible only in a condition of industrial democracy by workers' control.

The framework of the Syndicalist organisations of struggle is easily adaptable to the supreme task of taking over industry, and can evolve into the complex and refined system of control necessary for modern industry.

Miners would control the mines on behalf of society as a whole, textile workers the mills, railmen the railways. The factory would control affairs proper to the factory; the district of each industry the affairs of that industry in its own area.

What had been the National Federation of Labour, the grand army of workers welded together in the struggle against capitalism, would become the Economic Council of Labour - a delegate body to co-ordinate the work of the various economic syndicates.

Production would be for human needs and not for the profit of a few. The wage system would be abolished and, with a rise in techniques, there would come, not the present fear of redundancy and starvation, but a full and free life, such as we wage slaves have dreamed about but never yet tasted.

94

Nationalisation and the New Boss Class

Victory Over Toryism

The air raid sirens had hardly sounded the last all-clear when Britain was thrust into the hurly-burly of a General Election. Before the world's first atom bombs had fallen on Japanese cities, a Labour government with an overwhelming majority ruled the House of Commons, and when victory over Japan followed victory over Germany, a Labour Prime Minister, head of a victorious Labour Government, rose to tell a House of Commons packed to the roof with his jubilant comrades.

The road was now open, the way to the New Jerusalem was clear.

The older members of the Labour Party, who had canvassed on doorsteps after hard days in the factories, who had spoken from boxes on street corners to hostile or indifferent audiences, or to no audience at all, who had given precious coppers from their weekly doles to make this possible, were now about to see the fruit of their work. The hard work, the victimisations, the disappointments, were all as nothing in the bright promise of the new day.

But to millions of young Labour voters, casting a vote for the first time, such memories meant nothing. Their ideas were few and vague. They wanted a change and would give Labour a chance. They expected a better life than their fathers had had, but as to what they wanted the Labour Party to do, they were not sure. They had been too busy at war to formulate any ideas about peace.

In Search of a Programme

But were their elders, the pioneers, any clearer about Labour's programme? Peace has its victories, no less embarrassing than those of war. The Labour Government had a vast majority in Parliament and the support of the workers, expressed through big and wealthy trade unions.

The Tory enemy was cast down in defeat. Now to deliver the goods.

The Labour Government's economic programme was based on two principles - a give-away programme and state control of economic functions.

The first was expressed in family allowances, free health services, house, food and other subsidies.

The second principle led to state control of imports and exports, work licences, control of investment, direction of labour, price control and the nationalisation of some industries.

Most of this was uncertain ground to Labour M. P.s who were weekly swinging from the sombre deflation of Stafford Cripps to the cheerful inflation of the opposite wing. In the centre sat Attlee, not so much a leader as an umpire.

But on one plank the Labour Party stood with sure and confident feet - Nationalisation! Some of the other stuff was new, some was born of war and some had been opposed by the Labour Party 20 years earlier, but Nationalisation - the Party had been built on it.

The Necessity of Definitions

A word or a slogan may sound fine in a peroration, it may look well in a manifesto or on a banner, and you won't spoil the effect by not defining it, but when it has to be expressed in an Act of Parliament, you must know what you want. One is then in the position of a man who looks at a machine and says: Will it work?

Not all Labour speakers and writers were agreed on what was meant by Nationalisation. Some, like old Bob Smillie, drew loud applause by saying that they preferred the term socialisation. But this section was always vague and uncertain. The other opinion was definite. The Post Office was nationalisation, nearly every government in the world had nationalised the railways. . . .state pawnshops, water boards, even standing armies and floating navies were given as examples of Socialism. To them the world teemed with examples of nationalisation and its successes.

In the moment of decision the definite opinion usually prevails against the uncertain, so the post office and public utility school prevailed against the nebulous. The speeches of propagandists were screwed into lawyers' phrases and passed the House to cheers, the singing of the *Red Flag* and even a jig or two. Coal, gas and power were nationalised. Road transport, railways and the Bank of England were state-owned. State production was to follow. Here was the heart of the matter.

The Great Disappointment

The first results of nationalisation were disappointing but British workers were willing to be patient and give Labour a chance - a reasonable attitude for those who had voted Labour to power. But, as time went on, the first faults of the experiment appeared as permanent features. Still the Labour Government pressed on with plans for further nationalisation of industries, without considering any modification of the principle suggested by experience.

The third post-war General Election ended any further nationalisation, however, and it was the workers' disappointment with state ownership which then gave victory to the Tories. To some it seemed that a sigh of relief went up from the Labour Party ranks and it is certainly true that, since then, the party has shown no keenness for further state ownership. Plans for further blueprints and resolutions occasionally come from a section of the party, but they are not passed with any enthusiasm - rather are they repeated like an ancient creed.

On the other hand, definite opposition comes from the trade unions, who cry: First let us find out what is happening in the nationalised industries.

It is that problem which we should now consider. Left-wing apologists of state ownership claim that the new enterprises were, from the start, handicapped by having to pay fixed rates of interests on the capital assets of the previous owners. Certainly this is a handicap to the running of any industry and we have no sympathy with any shareholder, but other industries, privately owned, suffer the same burden. Further, these payments were long foreseen and successive Labour Party Conferences had rejected the principle of confiscation and renewed their belief in nationalisation with compensation by huge majorities.

To be quite fair, there was one serious economic difficulty with which the newly nationalised undertakings found themselves burdened....they came into being at the beginning of a long period of inflation. The public, workers and others, are apt to judge the nationalised commodity by a comparison with its pre-war price. Considering the changed value of money, the prices of some state commodities are not high - that is, compared with the prices of private enterprise. Electricity, post and telephones and railways show price increases much smaller than those of most other services and goods. On the other hand, coal shows a huge increase in price.

The Decline of King Coal

In Labour propaganda, coal was always the first subject for state ownership. Here, indeed, was a fruitful field for the great experiment. Not only Labour Party members, but many others, even Tories, were sympathetic to the idea. Certainly, Labour was confident it could make a success of state ownership in this, Britain's most important industry.

Now, alas, after a decade, nationalisation can deliver only limited supplies of coal at a greatly increased price, with the prospect of ever-increasing prices. Coal remains the last relic of wartime rationing. The rising cost endangers other industries, particularly steel (nearly three tons of coal are used in making one ton of steel), railways, gas, electricity and shipbuilding.

Coal, which had remained Britain's chief export, has ceased to be a true export and now coal is literally being carried to Newcastle from Poland the U. S. A.

The production figures of the coal pits are inflated by millions of tons of slate, rock and earth, while much valuable farmland is laid waste to produce open-cast coal of poor quality.

With the prospect of further reductions in coal production, industry - led by the Ministry - is turning from home-produced coal to imported oil for fuel. Trolley buses are replaced by diesels: railways are struggling with problems of oil fuel; industry, blocks of flats and offices are turning to oil for work and heat. Even power stations are changing over from coal to oil.

Oil or Coal?

More and more, Britain is having to turn her back on a home-produced commodity to favour a fuel which is social dynamite, whose very name conjures up the images of colonialism, intrigue and war. Britain, under either a Labour or a Tory government, intends to live on the exploitation of colonial workers.

With this increasing dependence on oil follows a more aggressive military policy to safeguard the oilfields and the oil routes. The blood shed in Cyprus and Suez has been shed for oil. The air and military bases stringing the Middle East are there for oil, to ensure it against foreign invasion or insurrection.

A change of party in office will make no difference. Both the major parties are pledged to the further use of oil. Indeed, it was the Labour Government which initiated the present changeover in industry. In 1946, the Labour Government formed a corps of technicians and propagandists to tour industry to persuade owners to turn from coal.

Both parties intend oil to be the life blood of industry and commerce, and both parties, should the occasion occur, will fight for oil.

Wars do not happen because politicians omit to ask one another to dinner, or because Churchill forgot to slap Stalin on the back. Wars are fought for sound economic reasons and the greatest of all these is oil.

Peace and Piety

A new foreign policy demands a new economic policy. However pious may sound the 'peace and friendship' slogans of a party's foreign affairs department, they will but act as a battle screen if behind them is the old economic policy.

The older ruling class was frank. . . .Trade follows the flag, they said. The armed forces and the diplomatic corps were to protect the capital investments and acquired natural resources of the British capitalists and the trade routes and stations needed fully to exploit them. The home resources of the country could be neglected for the more profitable degree of exploitation possible in a colonial country. The drive for profit became a drive to war. The lifelines of the country were threatened and export or die became export and die.

The extensive economic programme of the Labour Government was founded on the same basis as the old capitalist order and even sharpened the issue export or die! It was to be built on the Sterling Area, the British part of which was to be subsidised by Arab oil, Malayan tin and rubber, West African cocoa, South African gold and other colonially exploited commodities. Large, unprofitable areas were to be abandoned, but smaller, more intensely valuable areas retained. The trade routes, suspended on chains of islands and rocky 'protectorates' girdling the globe, were to be as jealously guarded as in the days of Victoria.

In office, Labour's foreign policy was: Keep the trade routes, export more, exploit the colonies and restore the traditional balance of power. This required peace-time conscription, increased armaments (with a trimming of the social services) and alliances with powerful nations having a similar economic basis.

Out of office, it was possible for Labour to resume its old platform slogans of peace, friendship, no conscription and reduction of armaments.

A return to office would, of course, put back on the shelf the lovely old sentiments of public meetings and banner headlines like last year's Christmas cards.

The East Wind of Economics

British capitalism's struggle for existence in the world's markets soon expressed itself at home in a contraction of the home market in an attempt to export more and cheaper goods. The workers in nationalised industries are not exempt from the effects of such a contraction. No industry is an island, independent of its fellows.

On the contrary, the workers in state industries are almost the first (after certain luxury trades, such as motor cars) to feel the effects of a planned 'recession' of economy.

It is now the intention of the British ruling class to cut back the post-war gains of the workers - a plan shared by the employers' organisations and the government. In this plan the state industries have early attention. Cheaper coal, electricity and transport are to be the basis of cheaper export commodities.

The new rulers, the controllers of the state enterprises, at once responded by pledging no further increases (for at least a year) in the price of their products. The railways, the Coal Board, the gas and electricity boards gave this assurance almost in unison.

Plainly, this meant no further wage increases for workers in those industries. Indeed, to be successful such a plan must ensure getting more work from the employees and real cutting down in the numbers employed.

The rulers of the state industries joined in the general plan with enthusiasm - were, indeed, the leaders in accepting it. Later they were joined by the employers' organisations, such as the Federation of British Industry. But, while the support of the F. B. I. and such bodies has consisted of very general statements, the state industries have given a very definite lead in 'recession.'

Whatever the social origin of the state executives - professors, trade-union officials or generals - they have given a public display of unanimity in the new economic policy.

So, far from being contenders against capitalism, the nationalised industries are proving to be its keystone.

They

That the nationalised industries should be used as the spearhead of an attempted offensive against wages would have seemed an odd idea to millions about ten or twelve years ago. Now, certainly to the workers in those concerns, the idea seems not at all remote. The state workers soon learned to regard the rulers of these industries as a new set of masters. Anyone who has travelled in South Wales or Durham since the war and has talked with miners there, must soon have noticed how conversation is continually directed against They, as it ever was.

Before state ownership, They were the coalowners and, more particularly, the owners' agents and colliery managers. Now, They are the National Coal Board, the mine agents and the mine managers, but the antagonistic attitude is the same - as though against a set of alien conquerors, like Anglo-Saxon peasants against Norman overlords.

Nor is the relationship of directors and managers with workers any better in the electrical power industry, gas, railways or airways. They are always the bosses, who must be watched, who must not know, who are opponents and must be fought - not merely to improve conditions a little, but even to retain what has already been won.

The one outstanding feature of the nationalised industries, from the day of their taking over, has been the complete lack of confidence between the boards and the workers and between managers and men.

It is important to realise that this is not something which has developed during the later years of state control, nor is one or another government responsible for it as an innovation. It was there from the day of birth.

The New Bosses

In the first years of the experiment, socialist workers in the State industries apologised for this relationship of enemies by saying it was teething trouble which would soon pass away. Alas! - even they were soon to admit that something was wrong with the set-up and that we have started off wrong. And that is where we must look - where we started off.

The composition of the Boards, the prescribed social relationship of management and workers, the economic philosophy whose fruit we now see. . . .all were there in the beginning, conceived by the Labour Government and cheered by the huge Labour majority in the House of Commons. It was no accident - right or wrong, the intention was there, the practical application of a social and economic school of thought.

The boards of the nationalised industries were all chosen by the one formula - a principle that ensured the continuance in power of the old ruling class and its continued prosperity, even under what might seem to be new conditions.

The new governors were wealthy business men, the kind the Labour Party in *Tribune* and *Forward* denounces as hard-faced capitalists, and Army generals of the type denounced by the *Daily Herald* as Colonel Blimps. To these was added a good sprinkling of trade-union leaders.

This applied not only to the boards of directors; the heads of department were chosen on the same principle. In the case of railways, particularly, a passing downstairs of a directive or enquiry from a general to another army officer, of lesser rank, looks little like a transport undertaking, but very much like a red-coated army on manoeuvres.

Old Bosses - New Powers

Below board level, below the heads of departments, the old managers remained, reinforced at various higher levels by the inevitable Colonel Blimps and numerous civilian heirs of the Old Pals' Act. No attempt was ever made - or intended - to draw a flood of managers from the ranks of the people, as had so often been boasted from Labour platforms. Nor was any attempt made to introduce a measure of industrial democracy as the beginning of a new social order in industry - another pompous boast of Labour speakers and writers.

Instead, while we see the old faces in power at the lower levels, backed by toadying foremen and workshop spies, the powers of the managers over labour have been greatly increased and reinforced by fear of the state's blown-up majesty.

Some poor folk may see in this a contradiction of Labour's policy. Not at all! All this is exactly in line with Labour's true policy. Every party, almost every sect and organisation, has two policies - one open and public, the other secret. The overt doctrine is usually vague and general, too frothy to be applied to life's problems. The secret doctrine is exact, worldly and very practical.

The non-public doctrine is not always written, or discussed in formal congresses, but has its greatest strength in the quiet places of the mind, and in the urgent desires of the controllers of organisations holding the double-doctrine principle. Thus, a religious body may preach voluntary poverty, humility, brotherhood and spiritual values, and condemn the use of force, yet its technicians may be devoted to the acquisition of wealth and social influence, be consumed by worldly pride and rely on a police force, and even an army, to maintain their wealth and power.

And it is always the secret, or non-propaganda, doctrine which is the more powerful, for it is the one men live by. How men act, what they do, is what they really believe.

Behind the platform and radio front of the Labour leaders is a wholly cynical attitude to life. While the most Left of its spokesmen condemn landlordism with the fervour of mediaeval peasants, they buy farms and landed property by outbidding the real farmer. With straight faces, they condemn business and the profit motive, while most of them are capitalists and in profit-grasping businesses, either on their own or as executives of big companies.

Their values are capitalist. As Sir Hartley Shawcross, Labour's leading lawyer, has recently said, no Labour Party member who **could** do so, would decline to send his sons to snob public schools such as Eton and Harrow, where a thorough training in capitalist values is assured.

As the leaders become more successful, their respect for the workers, the infantry of the Labour movement, becomes less, so that they no longer take great care to conceal their capitalist living from the members.

In truth, the object of the Labour Party has never been a classless, Socialist society. Its aim has always been to modify the ruling class. Now we see it controlled by capitalists (some of them big ones) peers of the realm, lawyers and other middle-class persons, together with aspiring politicians and trade-union leaders.

In the first stages of such a social movement, it often seems that a party is seeking to create a new ruling class, but, having achieved a certain measure of success, such a body usually joins forces with the old ruling class, thus gaining the experience of the old, as well as the more metallic prizes, and safeguarding itself against the subject class, who are likely to become rebellious.

The Labour Party, with its auxiliaries and the Communist Party - in short, the movement for state socialism - displays all the attributes of this counter-revolutionary social trend. The Labour Party began as a limited political expression of very orthodox trades unionism, but the middle-class careerists, with a thirst for power, were quick to see in its early small success a road to the top for themselves. The Macdonalds, the Snowdens and the Fabians were soon not only getting control of the party, but also developing their own ideal - the conquest and control of the worker.

Red Fabians

The main theme of this power-hungry band has always been, 'The workers do not understand what is good for them - they must be controlled and guided by us, for we alone understand their good.' The rise of dictatorships fascinated the middle class politicals. The British Fascist movement of Mosley began in the Midlands Labour Party, Mosley himself being a Labour Government minister, and Bolshevism has always fascinated them. Time and again they have opened their arms to the Communists - at least, to those who held power, only to be slapped in the eye by their arrogant Bolshevik comrades.

The respectable Fabians, persons like Shaw and the Webbs, loved the Russian dictatorship, seeing in it a sort of Fabianism, without the drawing room tea parties. Sidney Webb even saw the concentration camps, the torture and execution of political opponents, the secret police and the complete suppression of liberty as a new civilisation.

Paternalism

The middle-class Socialist idea of the Welfare State is based on a belief that the worker cannot be trusted to spend his own wages in a reasonable manner. Therefore, they say, an ever-increasing slice of that wage must be confiscated by income tax (P. A. Y. E. was welcomed and made permanent by the Labour Party) and by heavy indirect taxation, the sum resulting being used for the workers' benefit, after the expenses of government have been deducted.

No need to save for a rainy day - we'll take the money and pay you sickness benefit or public assistance. No need to save for old age - we'll save your money for you and pay you a pension. Father knows best.

But the welfare state also provides jobs for an ever-increasing army of 'intellectuals and professionals.'

The politically-aspiring middle class were without ideals or a programme at the end of the 19th century. At the same time, the workers were developing their ideas, in an attempt to give coherence to the struggle against the misery remaining from the industrial revolution. What more natural, then, than the permeation of the labour movement by these spiritually-barren shopkeepers?

Fraternity

The workers's social movement was not entirely starry-eyed, however. It was also very practical. Trade unions, mutual aid societies and factory clubs provided for sickness benefits, deaths, food supply for strikers, widows, orphans, loss of tools, protection against landlords. They even built hospitals. The early co-operative societies also expressed this urge towards fraternity.

But the developing labour movement was not satisfied with collecting pennies and giving to the needy, while tolerating capitalism - the cause of the misery. It was thinking its way towards a society in which such first aid would be unnecessary. The cause of this vast social misery, it was seen, was the concentration of property in the hands of a minority. At the same time, it was clear that society could not go back to peasant and artisan production, with a widespread distribution of private property.

It was understood that a redistribution of private ownership of the means of production would result in the loss of new industrial techniques and be followed by reduced production. It was seen that there could be little hope of a shorter working week or higher income by breaking up the factories, as peasants in revolt had broken up the big estates. Some form of collectivisation or social possession was needed. To retain large-scale production of industrial goods and services, but abolish their private ownership.

Some of the early aspirants of working-class liberation left it at that, but others attempted to give form and body to the idea - some by the idea of co-operatives, others by conceiving voluntary communes. The Syndicalists, however, wished to be more definite and developed the idea of Workers' Control of Industry.

When the middle-class and those they had been able to seduce by a dream of power had gained control of the labour movement, the idea of social ownership and democratic control was quickly buried. In its stead was put state control and state ownership, as in the Post Office.

Gradually, even in propaganda, socialisation was dropped and industrial democracy was supplanted by the man from Whitehall knows best. Worse still, the self-appointed schoolmasters of the labour movement let it be thought that the only alternative to private capitalism was their state capitalism and that they were the authors of all collectivism.

Today millions of workers do not know that the parent of collectivism was the prime movement of the workers, the struggling upwards of the socially-downtrodden, and not the self-styled 'intellectuals'.

Even in Soviet Russia, the classic land of nationalisation, this was the case.

Revolt in Russia

The Russian Revolution overthrew Tsarism in March,1917. It was followed in November, 1917, by the counter-revolution when the Bolsheviks seized power. The latter event, like most counter-revolutions, acted in the name of 'the revolution,' but the goal of the masses in revolt was the opposite of that established by the iron rule of Bolshevism. The Revolution sought to establish freedom of assembly, of speech, of person and of organisation. But these alone were not enough - such fine principles needed a sound economic basis.

This economic urge took form in the country by the peasant seizure of large estates and their division. The peasants, mostly under the leadership of the Social Revolutionary Party, made such a complete job of this land distribution that the Communist Party decided to support their slogans - after the event, for such seizure of land by the peasants was contrary to the Bolshevik programme, which had to be revised.

In industry the workers, influenced by Syndicalist ideas and organisations, organised on a factory basis and began to pass from part to complete control of the industrial unit and its collectivisation.

Maurice Dobb, a lecturer in economics at Cambridge University and a well-known Communist, confirmed this grass-roots movement towards socialisation in a book which was published, with Communist blessing, in the mid-1920's. In this book, *Russian Economic Development Since the Revolution, Dobb writes:-*

In the summer (1917) reports began to multiply of arrests of engineers by workers acting in the name of local Soviets, and the forcible expulsion of unpopular foremen.

We should recall that, at this time, the Soviets, or workers' councils, were mostly out of Communist control and the term had not then been perverted to its present meaning. Dobb further says:-

On June 1, a national resolution of the Executive Committee of the Soviets advised all industrial workers 'to create councils at the enterprises, the control embracing not only the course of work at the enterprise itself, but the entire financial side of the enterprise.'

But many workers were already going far beyond these directives and were turning the factories into collectives. Kronstadt, largely Syndicalist and Left Social Revolutionary, was prominent in this movement. Dobb reports:-

In the cable works the owner had actually been deposed by the local Soviet on the charge of trying to close down the plant and sell it to a foreign bank, and the concern was being administered by its factory committee.

In the Ukraine, where Syndicalism and Anarchism were strong, the movement developed rapidly. Dobb said that in July, 1917, a conference of factory committees threatened to remove owners and managers and elect working committees to run the factories, but at Kharkov locomotive works the workers had already arrested the owners and taken complete control. In Petrograd, where the employers threatened to close the factories, the workers replied by taking control. In Moscow, the leather workers acted in the same way.

Workers' Control in Russia

At Nikolaev in the south, shipyard workers took control of the enterprise, while in the Donbas coalfield the miners controlled the mines. From there, in October, 1917, General Kaledin wired to the Minister of War in Petrograd: At the moment the entire power has been seized by various self-appointed organisations which recognise no other authority than their own. The general, of course, referred to the factory and mine committees elected by the workers.

At the same time, the peasant movement for taking possession of the land continued to sweep over Russia, reaching almost 100 per cent. The land workers' movement was still not controlled by the Bolsheviks, who even to this day have remained at war with the peasants. The Peasants' Congress, called in the autumn, and meeting in the Petrograd Duma during November, 1917, showed that the Bolsheviks, after all their usual intrigue and gerrymandering, could muster only one-fifth of the delegates, while the Social Revolutionary Party had the vast majority.

The Peasants' Congress elected to the chair Maria Spiridonova, beloved revolutionary heroine and stalwart opponent of the Bolsheviks. The 'Land to the Peasants' movement swept onto completion with the success of the Anarchist peasant movement in the Ukraine, with which history forever couples the name of Nestor Makhno.

Throughout this great movement of social revolution, Lenin's thoughts were all of How can we, the Bolsheviks, gain the power and how can we keep it? Little else seems to have entered his mind for several years, except as consideration of minor factors as they affected the main idea. This is clearly shown in the printed writings and speeches of the great politician during those years. Even Dobb witnesses to this:-

The leitmotif running through the speeches and writings of Lenin in 1917 was the overshadowing importance of the political issue of the class which held the actual reins of power. For him this issue was paramount.

To Lenin, of course, as to all Communists, the use of the term class power always meant power for the Communist Party. Says Dobb:-

At any rate an immediate transition to a socialist economy was not on the agenda in the early months of the new Soviet regime. Immediate preoccupation was with the seizure of certain economic key positions to consolidate the political power. . . .But no sweeping measures of confiscation or nationalisation were immediately proposed. Rather was it a controlled or directed Capitalism, steered by such measures of economic control as had come to be the common stock-in-trade of belligerent governments, that was contemplated.

Lenin himself wrote that the new Bolshevik State power attempted to adapt itself to the conditions then prevailing as much as possible, as gradually as possible and breaking with as little of the past as possible. *(Lenin, Selected Works,* Vol.IX, p.284.)

The Bolshevik government nationalised the joint stock banks on December 17, 1917, because, said Dobb, of the strike by employees of the State Bank and civil servants.

To Turn the Tide

But the social movement did not stand still waiting for the Bolsheviks to hammer the last rivets in their dictatorship. The free socialisation movement went on sweeping Russia. There could be no political dictatorship if the workers and peasants held economic power. So the Lenin government took over the movement and turned it into state capitalism. The Communists never forgot the fright the people of Russia gave them and, since then, have used state capitalism to back up their political dictatorship.

But that even nationalisation is not fundamental to even present-day 'Communism' is proved by the frequent turns of the Communists towards private ownership of land and industry - the best example being their attacks on the Spanish Syndicalist movement. C. N. T - F. A. I., for its collectivisation in Spain during 1936-39. During that period, and before, the world Communist movement favoured private capitalism against social ownership. In Spain, they even used Russian tanks and artillery to destroy the collectives.

Only one principle has remained constant among the many twists and turns of Communist policy: how to get power and how to keep it.

The keen appreciation of Russian economic serfdom expressed by so many members of the Labour Party does not spring from ignorance, for in the Bolshevik dictatorship they see the fulfilment of their own desires. The Russian workers and peasants sought common ownership and democratic control of the means of production in their revolution. The principle they were establishing was essentially democratic; based on common ownership and workers' control, it was infinitely more democratic than anything known in Western Europe, being economic as well as social or political.

But what the Bolshevik counter-revolution established was a mixture of the State capitalism known to the West with Tsarist serfdom. The trade unions and peasant unions were dissolved, right of assembly denied, strikes suppressed and the worst 19th Century capitalist practices introduced.

That lack of control meant lack of ownership was soon evident, for Russian industry was clearly being run for the benefit of a privileged class. The workers were forced to toil harder than they had ever previously done under the Tsar - and as long ago as 1929 I heard Pollitt, leader of the British Communist Party, say that on returning to Russia after a few years' absence, he saw one man doing work previously done by three on the railways.

At the same time the standard of living of the peasants and workers was reduced. There has, for instance, been an almost constant shortage of food -

often amounting to famine - in Russia since the Bolsheviks gained power. Whenever they wished to discredit any of their fallen leaders, such as Malenkov recently, the man in question was accused of being responsible for the food shortage.

But shortage was only for the masses. . . .for the privileged class there has always been plenty. The Webbs, in their book *Soviet Communism, a New Civilisation,* said there was greater economic and social inequality in Russia than existed in Britain or the U. S. A.

Statism

Neither the Statism of the Labour Party nor that of the Communists is social ownership, they are State Capitalism. Under nationalisation, private capital is invested in a state-controlled industry and a fixed dividend paid, as in certain forms of private capitalist investment, the original owner is compensated, usually by being given blocks of state bonds, and the worker is exploited to continue the payment of rent, interest and profit. The worker in the state industry remains a wage slave, his wage regulated by the condition of the labour market, he has no more share in the management than have his brothers in I. C. I. or General Motors. He is still subject to the Boss, though usually to a brass-plated general instead of a traditional capitalist.

Nationalisation is not the invention of the Labour Party. The Tory Party, too, accepts State ownership. The Post Office, the telegraphs, cables and telephones were nationalised by Tories. There was no fundamental opposition to the nationalisation of the railways from the Tories, the issue being largely one of bargaining - the amount of dividend to be paid to the shareholders.

Capitalists, of course, often approve of nationalisation and public corporations when these suit their commercial or investment interests. The Port of London Authority, quoted by many Labour Party men as an example of Socialism, was formed by a capitalist government under the guidance of Lloyd George. The London Passenger Transport Board, an example of Socialism according to Herbert Morrison and others, was introduced by the Labour Government of 1929-31, but carried out by the following Tory governments.

Nor does the Labour Party believe in universal nationalisation. Already the responsible members of the party are scared of their previous programme and are even publicly crying Halt! to nationalisation. Sir Hartley Shawcross, seconded by Richard Stokes, was the first candid spokesman of the recantation.

Even those Labour M. P.s who have attacked Shawcross for his Halt to State Ownership cry, do it with so many ifs and buts that they cause one to doubt the difference between the policies of 'Right' and 'Left.'

The official policy of the Labour Party is now to be, in its chief economic plank, not nationalisation, but a vague programme of State ownership of shares in private companies, and its new pensions scheme is also to be based on capital investment. Even this is meeting with opposition from the Co-operative section of the Labour Party - a section powerful enough to have prevented the nationalisation of sugar and insurance during the last Labour Parliament - opposition based on its own interest in investment in these businesses.

It is already accepted among the Labour leaders that future Labour Governments shall be based on a society which has some industries under State capitalism, but most under private capitalism - with State shareholding in some of the latter. This policy is copied from the Tory act of State investment in the Anglo-Iranian Oil Company.

The Labour Party would be happy to lose nationalisation, if only they could do so on a dark night. With their new policy they also, of course, accept the continuance of social and economic inequality, the existence of a non-owning and a property-owning class, though some of the latter may own shares in State capitalist companies. They also accept that one class shall, at work, have no say in the management of industry, while the other class, including the Labour leaders themselves, shall have all power.

Gain or Loss?

State ownership had given no benefit to the workers, neither to those employed by the State, nor to those still working for the private form of capitalism. True, the miners' greatly-improved wages are cited as fruits of the new control, but the increase is due solely to the bigger demand for British coal and the general condition of the labour market. In any case, a sizeable increase in the miners' wage was bound to come, whatever the form of ownership.

As to the other State-owned industries, the reduction of working hours and wage increases have lagged behind those of private capitalism. Workers outside have set the pace in each wage round, with the State having to follow - outstanding examples of this being the Royal Dockyards and the Electricity Board's power stations, where the workers follow the gains made by the engineering unions in private capitalism.

The State industries find it most difficult to compete against the capitalist when recruiting labour. That is, surely, a formidable reply to those Socialists who claim that nationalisation improves the workers' wages and conditions.

As to conditions of work, in the State industries these are generally regarded as being much worse than those outside. (It should be noted that workers in State concerns speak of outside in much the same way as prisoners do.) The worst features are red tape, orders from above, bossing by officer relics of forgotten wars, repeated attempts to run these industries like a red-coated military tattoo and the general atmosphere of official form-filling irritation and pin-pricking.

No! Nationalisation is not Socialisation, but State Capitalism, the bastard beloved of the middle-class theorists who have captured the Labour movement, themselves neither fish, flesh nor fowl.

Socialisation, the ideal born of the early Labour movement, can only come from the workers and not from those who have a class interest in the preservation of capitalism. It is not State ownership, but the common, social ownership of the means of production, and social ownership implies control by the producers, not by new bosses. It implies Workers' Control of Industry - and that is Syndicalism.